PORSCHE
HIGH-PERFORMANCE
DRIVING HAND BOOK

Vic Elford

Motorbooks International
Publishers & Wholesalers ®

First published in 1994 by Motorbooks International Publishers & Wholesalers, PO Box 2, 729 Prospect Avenue, Osceola, WI 54020 USA

Motorbooks International books are also available at discounts in bulk quantity for industrial or sales-promotional use. For details write to Special Sales Manager at the Publisher's address

Library of Congress Cataloging-in-Publication Data

Elford, Vic.
Porsche high-performance driving handbook / Vic Elford.
p. cm.
Includes index.
ISBN 0-87936-849-8
1. Automobile driving. 2. Porsche automobile. I. Title.
TL152.5.E39 1994
629.283—dc20 93-34450

On the front cover: Vic Elford stand alongside a Porsche Carrera 4 Wide Body. *Anita Elford*

On the back cover: Vic Elford driving a Porsche 917 at the 1971 12 Hours of Sebring. *Leonard Turner*

Printed and bound in the United States of America

Contents

"I've known Vic since 1968 when I almost signed to drive in the Cooper Formula 1 team with him. Prior to that, Vic was world renowned for his prowess as a rally driver. He then got the opportunity to show his versatility by driving in Formula 1 and followed up by becoming one of the world's top sports car drivers in the legendary Porsche 917, where I got to know him better.

"Since his retirement from professional racing I've had the pleasure of working with him at the Porsche Owners Driving School where he did an excellent job administrating the program. We worked at diverse venues throughout the United States, from Candlestick Park to Sebring.

"To drive a car well has to be learned from someone with a special talent of being able to impart that knowledge gained over the years.

"Vic Elford has that talent."

Derek Bell
Five-time winner of the 24 Hours of Le Mans,
two-time winner at Daytona, and twice World Sportscar champion.

"There is no driver better qualified than Vic to write a book on how to drive a Porsche—or anything else for that matter. The only driver to successfully switch from driving 911 rally cars on snow and ice, to racing 240mph Porsche 917s at Le Mans—in the rain, fog and night.

"This book will tell you all that you need to know."

Brian Redman
Porsche and Ferrari factory driver,
U.S. Formula 5000 champion.

Martina Navratilova and myself at the Porsche Owners Driving School.

"I always knew how to go fast but Vic taught me how best to stop—a very essential part of safe driving. Thank you Vic."

Martina Navratilova
Arguably the greatest women's international tennis champion of all time and Porsche Owners Driving School graduate.

About the Author

Vic Elford was thirteen years old when his father took him to see the first British Grand Prix at Silverstone after the Second World War. That day he decided he wanted to be a racing driver, a ridiculous notion at the time, since only wealthy young gentlemen could afford to drive racing cars. But throughout school and college the dream stayed alive, and he eventually got his foot on the bottom rung of the ladder and started the long climb to the top.

Certainly other drivers have been more successful than Vic in terms of races and championships won. There have been great Formula 1 champions, Indy drivers, stock car drivers, great rally drivers. But no other driver in the history of the sport has had success in so many varied disciplines.

Vic was the first British driver really to learn how to drive on ice and snow, which he put to good use by being the first person to win the Monte Carlo Rally for Porsche. He followed that up a week later by winning Porsche's first 24 Hour race at Daytona. Those two events marked the start of a long love affair and almost lifetime devotion to the German marque.

As a result of that experience he asked Bill France if he could try a stock car and came back to Daytona Speedway the following year to finish eleventh in the 500! Two years later he might have done even better. Seventh in his 125 miler, he was running seventh in the Daytona 500 when the crew let him run out of gas with about four laps to go!

In his first Grand Prix he finished fourth, even though he was driving the slowest car in the field and started last but one, thanks to his ability to drive in the rain.

Vic also finished seventh in an outdated Cooper-Maserati in the Monaco Grand Prix just months after winning the Monte Carlo Rally, becoming the only driver ever to have started both events, let alone finish both and win one.

He had countless victories in international rallies, world championship sports car races, and other branches of the sport, and he is still winning today in vintage racing, where he drives McLarens, Ferraris, Pontiac Trans Ams, and other cars.

No matter what you drive, probably no other driver in the history of motorsports is more qualified to offer advice on how to do it.

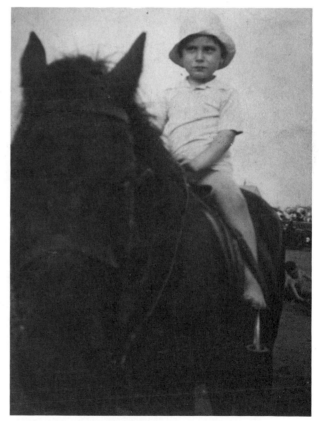

My first one-horsepower experience in England at the age of four. Vic Elford collection

5

Porsche 917, Daytona, 1971
*Many years later I had graduated to the 650hp of the
Porsche 917, here seen battling with two Ferrari 512s on
the banking at Daytona in 1971.... Vic Elford collection*

Porsche 917/30, Hockenheim, 1973
*...And ultimately the 1250hp of the fabulous Porsche
917/30 at Hockenheim. Eberhard Strähle*

Foreword
by David Hobbs

Although I have known Vic for over twenty-five years and have known of him for thirty years or so, it was not until I read his manuscript and the memories came flooding back that I again realized just how incredibly successful and comprehensive his rally and racing career had been. It also reminded me of some less than charitable thoughts I had held for "Quick Vic" many years ago as he made the switch from rally to race driver and purloined some drives that I was hoping for! How positively churlish.

Back in those "good old days" only ability counted to get drives. Mind you, a bit of astute politicking on the side never did any harm! But apart from the rich drivers Vic mentions, who usually drove their own cars, the "buy-a-ride era" had yet to dawn. Drivers were contacted regarding a certain drive or even a season and were offered money for their services. Now when contacted, drivers are expected to have some ability and *lots* of money!!

The point of this digression is that Vic got where he is by sheer raw talent. In his case it was exceptional talent and hard work. To win the Monte Carlo Rally in the depths of winter over the dark and incredibly dangerous mountain passes of the Alpes Maritime and then proceed to come in seventh in an uncompetitive car just five months later in the Principality's Formula 1 Grand Prix is without a doubt an outstanding achievement in racing that no one else has ever even come close to emulating.

Vic also won the Monte Carlo Rally and the Daytona 24 Hours within a couple of weeks of each other! He won most of the great sports car classics that every driver dreams of winning: Nürburgring (where he is the only driver *ever* to have won six major events), the Targa Florio, Sebring.... All the races that I myself had wanted to win so desperately. To make matters worse, he was a multiwinner in many cases! When you add in Trans-Am, Can-Am, and Formula 1, it is just about as diverse a career as possible.

This book, however, is not about "Vic Elford, racing driver," but about "Vic Elford, instructor." It disseminates some of that vast store of rare qualities that made him what he was, to you, thereby increasing your knowledge and interest in all facets of driving. He discusses many issues in this book that are normally either ignored or taken for granted, such as the chapters on smoothness, comfort behind the wheel, and braking and acceleration techniques—the whole gamut of driving. Every chapter is illustrated by a wonderfully delicious anecdote of a race or rally where the particular point in question is highlighted.

Not so long ago Vic and I worked together on a ride and drive program for BMW North America directed at its dealer network personnel. The program was run by the Skip Barber organization, and Vic and I were the two senior instructors. We criss-crossed the country visiting most of the better-known race venues in the states. The program was simple but effective—and I might add it sadly illuminated the abilities of the average road driver. As dealers and salespeople for the "ultimate driving machine," one might have expected them to be a bit more above average. As I said, illuminating!

The racetracks themselves were marked by cones for braking, entry, apex, and exit points in order to make life easier for the drivers. However, before getting onto the track we had a session with track diagrams and a few words from the instructors. I was struck then by Vic's conscientious approach to the task and his obvious teaching abilities. He made his points clearly and concisely and carried this theme throughout the program. Vic was a real stickler for detail, making sure his drivers were seated just right in the car and making sure that they all took absolute note of everything he was saying to them.

Since that time Vic went on to create the Porsche Owners Driving School for Porsche Cars North America. This was a full-time occupation for him, so he further honed his educational skills.

Driving education in general is poor the world over and is almost nonexistent in the United States, where driving is regarded as almost a divine right. Road safety, therefore, is usually not achieved by education but by legislation, some of it very flawed legislation. It would be comforting if the 90 million or so drivers on our roads had at least some idea of how to *drive* rather than just how to get from point A to point B.

This book will certainly go a long way toward alleviating that problem. For those who really do intend to improve their driving habits and skills, this book is a must. It is full of tricks of the trade, essential information on how to handle certain situations, great tips on car control in all conditions, and just plain common sense. It is also a damn good read! Full of some of the most fascinating experiences of one of the world's most diverse and successful drivers.

In 1970, the BOAC 1000km at Brands Hatch in England was wet. And I mean wet! For some reason I was not taking part but watching Vic Elford in the Porsche Austria 917 and Pedro Rodriguez in the Gulf-Wyer 917 duke it out. It was a breathtaking display of car control...that went on for six hours! My memories of that titanic struggle in the rain are still vivid and Vic's performance conjures up a line from Crocodile Dundee..."Now that's a driver."

Now read on!

David Hobbs
Former World Class Formula 1, Sportscar and Trans-Am driver, now ESPN motor racing commentator.

Preface

This is not the first book written on the subject of high-performance driving. It will probably not be the last.

So why bother?

Over twenty years ago, I remember being driven by an elderly German driver in a Mercedes 180 taxi from the Nürburgring through the Eiffel mountains to Bonn airport. The driver had absolutely *no idea* how to drive, and on corner after corner we were saved from catastrophe by the inherent capabilities of the car.

Today's cars have made such strides in road-holding, acceleration, and braking that it almost seems superfluous to be able to drive well. The car can do it all. Right?

Wrong!

With certain high-tech racing exceptions, the car can only respond to the input of the driver; it cannot do anything on its own. The better and more refined the demands of the driver, the better the car will respond. Under any given circumstances, the better the driver, the higher the speed he or she can drive at, the more pronounced the comfort, and above all, the greater the margin of safety.

This book is dedicated to Porsche drivers and all the other drivers who put quality and performance first—although you do not have to drive a Porsche to benefit from the knowledge and experience that I will try and share with you.

No driving handbook has ever dealt with every type of driving before. Many authors have offered books oriented toward racing, but none has covered the complete spectrum of driving as this book does. From driving on the high-speed autobahn to the delicate handling of a Porsche 911 on snow and ice, from off-road driving to accident avoidance in a school zone—whatever you drive, wherever you drive it, young or old, experienced or debutante, there is something in this book for you.

Porsche poster celebrating my winning the Monte Carlo Rally in 1968. Porsche

Acknowledgments

I know it sounds a little stereotyped and trite in today's world, but I really do have to start by thanking my parents. My mother was an orphan when she was twelve, and my father was already alone and earning his own living when he was eleven. For them, the idea that one could even imagine driving racing cars for a living, unless one had been born a millionaire and didn't need to make a living, was simply inconceivable. They had worked hard and sacrificed much in order for me to graduate from engineering college.

And then I announced that I was going to be a racing driver!

My early years in the seat beside the wheel and then in the seat behind the wheel they accepted with a grim resignation, because at least I still had a "real" job as an engineer.

Then suddenly one night they were listening to a live radio report (cable TV did not exist in those days and in England the only TV was the BEEB, or BBC) from the Mont Ventoux hill climb in France, one of the special stages of what for me was the ill-fated 1967 Monte Carlo Rally.

In the voice of the probably bored, at least to start with, BBC announcer, who would no doubt have preferred being home in front of a nice log fire...

"...and I see the lights of the next car approaching...and now another set of lights coming up behind at tremendous speed...they are catching the car in front...they are going to overtake...it's not possible...there is no room to get by on this snow-covered road...but they've done it, they've gone by the other car...and...and...it's Britain's Vic Elford...in the beautiful new Porsche 911 flying toward the summit...."

We didn't win—that year—but suddenly I had my two most ardent supporters for the rest of my career.

Many other people deserve recognition, and I have tried to list them here. Their names are listed in no particular order, and if I have forgotten anyone, I apologize.

They say that the first shall be last and the last shall be first. The first and last person involved in this book is Michael Dregni, editor in chief of Motorbooks International. Having just written a foreword for another Motorbooks International book, *Porsche Legends* by Randy Leffingwell, I asked Michael if he would be interested in republishing, in English, the autobiography that I had written in French nearly twenty years ago.

The reply was a simple (but polite), "No thanks." He then went on to suggest, "But perhaps with all of your Porsche background and teaching experience you could write a 'How to Drive a Porsche' book?" So I did, and here it is.

The following people also helped make this book possible and deserve thanks:

Alec Rhodes, with whom I did my first rallies as a codriver, stuffed into the passenger seat of an MG TF.

David Seigle-Morris, who was looking for a codriver for international rallies when Alec decided to sell his MG and get married.

Ken Piper, who drove a DKW, and David Blackburn, the managing director of DKW in Britain, who gave me my first real chance to try and show what I could do. And all the mechanics at DKW who worked after hours with no pay to keep my car running!

My friend John Sprinzel, whom you will meet later.

Graham Robson, journalist and manager of Triumph Motorsports, who having been passed in the night by—for once a flying not crashing—DKW, gave me a chance in the Triumph "works" team.

Walter Hayes, for his confidence in incorporating me into the Ford of Britain rally team.

Bill Barnett, of Ford, for all his support during what were often difficult times for both of us.

John Aldington and his father Bill, the British Porsche importers, who gave me the opportunity to contest the British Touring Car racing championship in a Porsche 911. I won the championship for them, for me, and for Porsche.

Richard Petty, who is perhaps responsible for my still being alive today.

"Old" Bill France, with whom I always had a great relationship from the first time I ever went to Daytona.

Jim Hall, who out of the blue asked me to drive the fabulous Chaparral 2J "vacuum cleaner" in the Can-Am, as well as his Chaparral Camaro in Trans-Am.

Most especially, thanks to all those people at Porsche whom I counted as my friends for so many years:

The beautiful Evi Butz, whom many of you now know as Mrs. Dan Gurney, but who for years, along with Thora Hornung, was "Miss Fixit" in the racing/public relations/customer relations departments at Porsche in Stuttgart.

The engineers, many of whom you will meet in these pages: Hermann Briem, Norbert Singer, Peter Falk, Helmut Flegl, Helmuth Bott. And perhaps the greatest automobile engineers of all time, Dr. Ferdinand Porsche and Dr. Ferdinand Piëch, along with all the mechanics who looked after the cars so lovingly, and everyone else at Porsche AG.

David Stone, who for so long was my rally co-driver and contributed so much to my success in that field.

And to the one single man who was responsible for the fact that I was able to write this book, Baron Fritz Huschke von Hanstein and his lovely wife Ursula.

President Fred Schwab and the staff of Porsche Cars North America and Porsche AG and Leo Mehl, of Goodyear Tire and Rubber Company also contributed in no small way to making this book possible.

Last, but not least, to my marvelous wife Anita, who has been subjected to countless proofreadings over the last six months. They were made all the more valuable by the fact that she also used to drive in rallies and hill climbs in both France and her home country of Belgium years ago, so at least she had a vague idea of what I was trying to say.

Thanks to all of you.

Vic Elford
Chevalier de l'Ordre National du Mérite

Porsche poster celebrating my winning the Targa Florio in 1968. This was the sole Porsche poster devoted to a driver rather than a car. Porsche

and her home country of Belgium years ago, so at least she had a vague idea of what I was trying to say.

Thanks to all of you.

Vic Elford
Chevalier de l'Ordre National du Mérite

Chapter 1

Comfort

The place: Sicily
The time: 1968
The occasion: The 52nd running of the "Targa Florio"

Ever since cars were built, men—and (more and more) women—have raced them.

The Targa Florio was the last surviving true road race, dating from the beginning of the century. It consisted of ten laps of a 45-mile circuit traced on narrow, twisty, mountain roads running through the landscape of the Italian island of Sicily.

A year earlier in 1967, after my first rallies in a Porsche 911 (the Tour of Corsica and Monte Carlo), Porsche racing director Huschke von Hanstein had asked me, "Have you ever thought about road racing?" What a question. When I replied that I had thought of little else since I was thirteen years old, he said, "OK, I think you had better start with the Targa Florio, it is like rallying in a racing car."

So after a few laps in a 911 to start learning the circuit, I found myself behind the wheel of my first ever real race car at 6 a.m. one morning. The car was a Porsche 906, and I remember wondering how in the world anyone could drive such a monster on a racetrack let alone around the mountains of Sicily. Huge front fenders reduced the frontal vision to the point where it was like looking through a funnel to just a narrow angle of road in front of the hood. But before the end of my first lap, I felt at home—and comfortable.

In the race itself I drove a Porsche 910 with Jochen Neerpasch. With smaller wheels and fenders, it had better visibility and was more maneuverable than the 906, and we finished third, behind two 2.2-liter Porsche 907s.

Now, a year later in 1968, I roared away from the start line in a Porsche 907. The village of Cerda was already behind me as I braked hard

Targa Florio, 1968
Umberto Maglioli and myself moments after our historic Targa Florio victory in 1968. After a first lap delay due to an ill fitting wheel lug nut, an unscheduled pit stop in the mountains, an off-road excursion caused by the wheel problems and a further pit stop to rectify those problems, I started the second lap of the ten-lap, 450-mile race eighteen minutes behind the leader. In a never-say-die drive, I fought back to win by over two minutes. Porsche, famous for their victory posters, dedicated this one to Elford—it is the only Porsche poster ever that shows only the driver, not the car. Rainer Schlegelmilch

12

Porsche 910, Targa Florio, 1967
My first "real" race in a "real" race car: The 1967 Targa Florio, finishing third with Jochen Neerpasch in a

Porsche 910. The smaller wheels and front fenders made the car infinitely more driveable than the 906 that I had used for practice. A. Giuliano

and changed down to second gear for the tight left hairpin corner that would lead me up into the mountains. My foot came off the brake and onto the throttle pedal, the engine revved—and the car just coasted slowly to a halt!

Assuming the clutch or transmission had broken, I unbuckled and climbed out only to find that the right rear wheel had almost come off. (It was later discovered that a badly machined center lock wheel nut from an outside supplier did not match the wheel and had simply undone itself.) Spectators clambered down from the bank beside the road to help. I didn't even need to get the jack out—they lifted the car bodily while I tightened the wheel!

I strapped myself back in and set off again with a vengeance. High in the mountains, all the serious teams had established an unofficial pit area, and I stopped briefly to have the wheel changed (but not the wheel nut as they did not have any).

Ten minutes later the same wheel nut undid itself again, but this time it was on a fast downhill

section, and as I lost power I also lost control of the car and slid off the road against a curb, puncturing a front tire! Again the spectators came to my rescue, lifting the car so that I could put the Goodyear space-saver spare on the front and retighten the rear.

After a further stop at the main pits to change all four wheels and wheel nuts, I started the second lap eighteen minutes behind the leader. Throwing caution to the winds, I drove like I had never driven before and probably never have since. Victory, I was sure, had eluded us, but I was determined to at least set a new lap record. I did—no less than four times—with each lap faster than the last.

I began making up time in great chunks. My codriver, Umberto Maglioli, kept the ball rolling during his three laps in the middle, and I took over again for the last three. As I passed the halfway pit area on the last lap, one of the German Porsche mechanics was bounding up and down brandishing a huge sign telling me that the last time past the start/finish line I had taken the lead.

13

Porsche 908/3, Targa Florio, 1971
The atmosphere of the Targa Florio is captured in this shot with families watching from their vantage points.

Here I was in the Porsche 908/3 in 1971. Vic Elford collection

Porsche 907, Targa Florio, 1968
Background scenery on the Targa Florio...the sleepy little town of Cerda in the background as I head up into the

mountains en route to one of my most pleasing victories. Werkfoto Porsche

Porsche 907, Targa Florio, 1968
All dressed up to watch Sunday's race! Despite the month of disruption to their quiet lives, the Targa Florio *was the social event of the year for many Sicilians.* Werk-foto Porsche

---

I felt so comfortable, so much at one with the car, that I almost wished the race would go on forever!

Through the villages of Collesano and Campofelice, where only a little over half an hour earlier the populace had been savoring the prospect of an Italian victory for Alfa Romeo, I stayed at full speed. I directed every ounce of concentration to keeping the car on the slippery, tortuous road, and I was unaware of the glasses of wine being raised to this crazy Englishman who had brought

Porsche back from the jaws of defeat. I was hot (the scirocco wind was blowing across the Mediterranean from North Africa), tired (I had been at the wheel for more than four of the last six hours), thirsty, and almost exhausted from the physical and nervous effort.

Still taking each corner at the limit as I swooped down out of the mountains for the last time, I reached the narrow road that ran straight along the sea front where for five miles the pounding wind buffeted the car left and right at 175mph. Through the last series of corners to the start/finish area where everyone—even the Italians— was going wild. I felt so comfortable, so much at one with the car, that I almost wished the race would go on forever!

Porsche 908/3, Targa Florio, 1971
Despite the proximity of spectators to the race cars, the Targa Florio had an enviable safety record, although only God knows why. Here I was in the Martini Racing

Team Porsche 908/3 almost running over people's toes as I swept through a corner in the 1971 event.... Werkfoto Porsche

Porsche 911RS, Targa Florio, 1973
...And here a 911RS follows a 914 while spectators line the road. Werkfoto Porsche

Targa Florio, 1968
Co-driver Umberto Maglioli and I savor the pleasure of victory in 1968. Ignacio Giunti and Nanni Galli, whose

Alfa Romeo appeared to have the race in hand after my first-lap troubles, stand by our sides. I was determined to win that race. Eric della Faille

The Importance of Comfort

When you see a driver exit a car hot and tired after an arduous race you might think that comfort is of little importance. Nothing could be further from the truth! European or world championship rallies often call for virtually nonstop, almost flat-out driving for twenty-four hours or more at a time. Even long-distance sports car or 500-mile races may see drivers called upon to stay at the wheel for four hours.

When you drive a Porsche, every moment of the time spent behind the wheel should be a pleasure. On the other hand, if you are not comfortable, driving becomes a chore, attention and concentration can wander, and in the extreme you might find yourself in an accident.

I hate the cold and for me anything under 75 degrees Fahrenheit is cold, so you can imagine how comfortable I was when Ford once sent me to practice for the Swedish Rally, where the temperature was 25 degrees below zero, in a car *with no heater*!

Targa Florio, 1969
Three years later Ignacio Giunti was tragically killed in Argentina. I was determined to win the once-only Giunti Memorial Trophy presented to the driver with the fastest lap in the Targa Florio race, in memory of my friend. Here I accept the trophy from Giunti's mother at the prize-giving ceremony. Werkfoto Porsche

Sit as low as is reasonably possible in your car—so long as you can still see over the steering wheel.

Seating Position

Have you ever bought a good-looking, expensive pair of shoes and then found the first time you go out in them that they are so uncomfortable that it takes all the pleasure out of wearing them?

The same can be true for a car. If you are not comfortable driving that beautiful Porsche, even a short journey will take on the aspect of a nightmare. Conversely, a little time spent preparing will make each moment behind the wheel such a joy that you will spend as much time there as possible!

During 1990–1992, while I was running the Porsche Owners Driving School that I created for Porsche Cars North America, I noticed that the vast majority of drivers started by sitting much too high in the car. They were not happy unless they could see the extremities of both front fenders, as well as the ground about three feet in front of the car. In fact, you should learn, even without being able to see them, exactly where the front fenders are. Within reason, the lower you can sit in the car the better. As long as you can still see over the steering wheel—not through it—the more comfortable you will be. The lower you sit, the better you can feel the *balance* of the car.

Within reason, the lower you can sit in the car the better. The lower you sit, the better you can feel the balance of the car.

So, if you have a car in which the seat height is adjustable, start by putting it as low as it will go. You can still see over the wheel? Good.

Now adjust the fore and aft positioning of the seat until, with brake and clutch pedals fully depressed, you still have a comfortable bend in the knees. Nothing is more uncomfortable—or frightening—than pushing to the limit of your fully extended leg and finding that you are still not quite at the limit of brake or clutch movement! If your car has power-assisted brakes, make sure you do this with the engine running, otherwise you will not get the full extension of the brake pedal!

The next step is to adjust the rake of the seat back so that with a comfortable angle, with your head in a relaxed position (not straining your neck

18

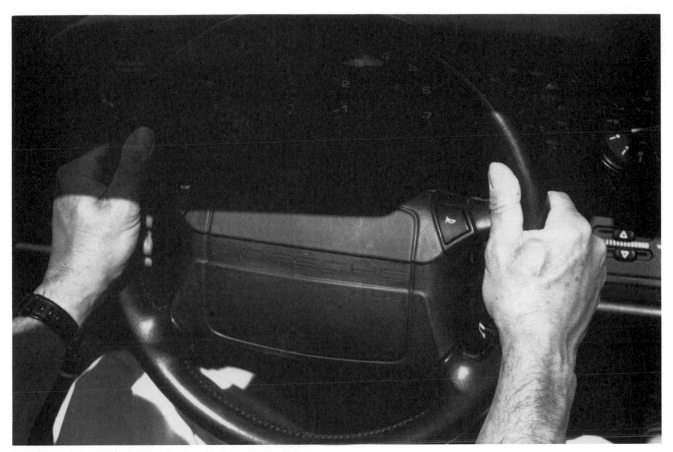

Place your hands at the 3 o'clock and 9 o'clock positions.
For open-road driving you should rarely, if ever, need to
change the position of the hands on the wheel.

muscles to hold it up straight), and with your hands at approximately the 3 o'clock and 9 o'clock positions on the steering wheel, your elbows are slightly bent. (The 3 o'clock and 9 o'clock positions may not be exact but will depend on the position of the spokes of the steering wheel.)

Depending on what your driving plans are, you might even think about purchasing a wraparound aftermarket seat, which although more difficult to get in and out of, will hold you even more firmly in place than the original seat. Many companies offer such products and can be found in the Porsche Club magazine *Panorama*.

Steering Wheel Position

If the steering wheel is adjustable, position it as high as possible, but make sure that you can still see over it. At the same time, if you have a tilt wheel, adjust the angle of the wheel so that it is roughly perpendicular to an imaginary line drawn from your shoulders to the wheel center.

There are two schools of thought about the placing of the thumbs relative to the spokes of the steering wheel. If you are driving a modern ground effects racing car, then you will almost certainly need the additional leverage provided by hooking your thumbs over the spokes. However, for normal road driving and especially for driving on poor surfaces such as snow and ice, gravel, off-road, or other conditions that make rapid, violent, and large steering inputs necessary, it may be better *not* to use this approach, but to lay the thumbs along the rim of the wheel. In the event of a violent steering wheel kickback, this position will help prevent an excruciatingly painful (and I speak from experience) dislocated thumb!

With the body and arms now correctly positioned, you should be able to make a complete half turn of the steering wheel without pulling your shoulders away from the backrest. Indeed, the upper hand should be able to make almost three-quarters of a turn without the shoulder moving forward.

If you drive a Porsche, chances are that your steering wheel is already leather covered, which in my opinion gives the best and most comfortable grip. If you don't yet own a Porsche and your car

19

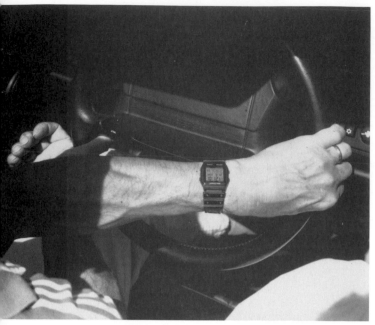

Hand position for a comfortable half turn of the steering wheel.

Hand position for almost three-quarters of a turn.

Make sure you can turn the steering wheel a good half or even three-quarters of a turn without dragging your shoulders away from the seat as I am purposefully doing here.

has a plastic steering wheel, you might want to have it covered in leather to make it more comfortable. Plastic steering wheels are often too thin to give a really comfortable grip, so while you are at it, you might want to have it slightly padded as well.

The ultimate modification, of course, is to replace the original steering wheel with an aftermarket one. A number of companies make some excellent products, and you might find what you want in your local accessory store. Better still, go to the experts where if the wheel you ordered is not quite what you expected, you can return it or exchange it and be sure you have the right one for you.

If, because of your physical build, there is a conflict between the seat position for legs and arms and it is impossible to get the exact positions shown above, *the arms should have priority*.

Gearshift Position

In a Porsche, once you get the body, hand, and arm positions adjusted as above, you will find that the gear lever falls perfectly to hand. Or to be even more graphic, just letting go of the steering wheel will allow the hand to fall naturally onto the gear lever.

If you drive something other than a Porsche, and you find yourself having to reach for the gear lever, you might need to modify the lever itself or even have a new one made, but the ergonomics of virtually all modern cars are so good that there is little likelihood of that being necessary.

Leg and Pedal Position

If, having done all that, your legs are bent slightly more than shown—no problem. If it means that now you cannot reach the pedals then you may have to visit your Porsche dealer or your local service station for a little minor surgery to the car. If you are a competent mechanic, you can even do it yourself at home. By "it" I mean adding blocks to the surface of the pedals so that you can fully depress them as described above.

In theory the block for each pedal—accelerator, brake, and clutch—should be the same thickness so that the pedals keep their same positions relative to each other as the original. (If you own a Porsche 928 then you are in luck as it is one of the few cars in the world with pedals that are adjustable relative to the seating position.) Some aftermarket suppliers even offer a complete replacement pedal assembly for 911 models that can help solve this problem. However, do not rush out and do this right now—wait until you have read chapter 8!

In addition to the throttle, brake, and clutch pedals, most Porsches have an additional pedal to the left of the clutch. The Europeans call it simply a footrest. Americans often refer to it by the quaint name of "dead" pedal, which does not appeal to me very much, so in this book I will call it a footrest. Whenever the car is moving your left foot should be firmly planted on the footrest. The knee should be slightly bent so that you can force yourself lightly but firmly back in the seat, and the left foot should be able to simply slide to the right when it is needed on the clutch pedal.

If your car does not have a footrest it is well worth the effort and minimal investment to fabricate and fit one. It is all part of the comfort package that will help you be a better driver.

Last, but by no means least, make sure your mirrors are properly adjusted. You may have to move them three or four times to get them right, but you should be able to see clearly what is behind you with just a flick of the eyes, not an exaggerated movement of the head!

In a racing car, everything is designed to be almost infinitely variable. First the seat is molded around the driver, then the position of the steering wheel, pedals, and even gear shift lever are adjusted and tailored just for him or her. Obviously this is not possible in a production car, but again, aftermarket sources can probably help if you really have problems.

Comfort can be defined as when the driver becomes an almost integral part of the car. The only body parts that can really move are the arms and legs. Maureen Magee

Seatbelts and Driving Harnesses

Most states and indeed most countries worldwide now require the use of seatbelts by drivers and front seat passengers although neither their use, nor the enforcement of their use, is as high as it should be.

Seatbelts save lives by keeping you inside the rigid, central structural capsule of a car in the event of an accident. Yet almost daily I read in my local newspaper of teenagers (especially) being killed, having been ejected from their vehicle in an accident. Frequently they are single-vehicle accidents. All too often they are caused by a moment's lack of attention or lack of appreciation of what the car can or cannot do and how to get out of a difficult situation. Many would have been survivable accidents, if only the victims had been wearing seatbelts.

Many years ago, before cars were fitted with safety belts as standard, a friend of mine was driving along Knightsbridge, a well-known, fashionable London street at about 30mph. Seeing another car approach down a side street at high speed he slammed on the brakes to avoid an accident. In fact, there was no accident as the other driver stopped before reaching the intersection. My friend's wife was taken by surprise and died from

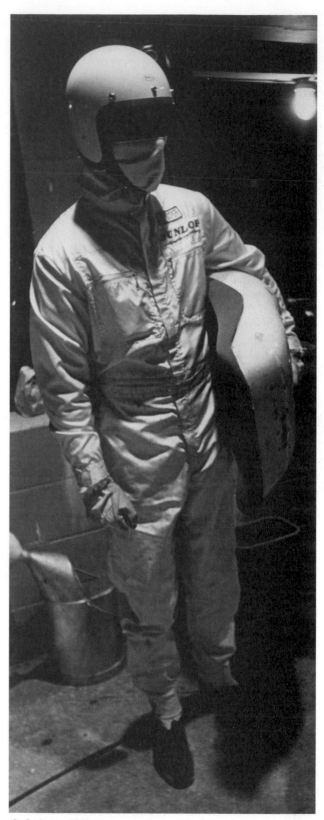

Sebring, 1968
Holding my own personal seat molded to my body, I await my turn on the night shift at Sebring. Each driver had his own seat, which fitted into the rigid seat shell inside the Porsche 907. Dave Friedman

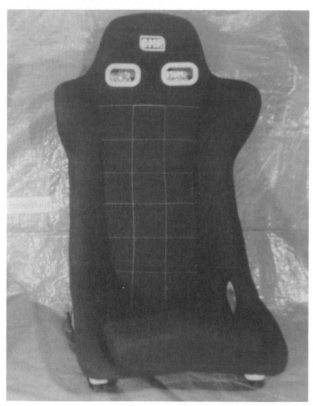

Wraparound seats should hold the entire body, especially with lateral support stretching all the way down to the thighs. This is one of many available.

22

Cooper F1, Nürburgring, 1968
Comfort really is important...even in Formula 1 even just waiting for the rain to stop at the Nürburgring!
Jutta Fausel

injuries received when her head hit the windshield, a tragedy that would certainly have been avoided in a car with seatbelts.

Why is it considered so macho to show what a big man or woman you are by not wearing belts? In fact, wearing them may not only save your life in the event of an accident, it will also help to hold you firmly in position in the driver's seat, giving you much more positive control of the car. No wasted energy or concentration trying to avoid being thrown around while driving quickly. Feet and hands are free to concentrate 100 percent on getting the best out of the vehicle.

If you watch NASCAR, IndyCar, or Formula 1 racing on ESPN, note how carefully the crew and the driver make sure that the driver is strapped in so tightly he or she becomes one with the car. Have you ever watched with amazement as a strapped-in driver walks away from a racing crash that reduced the car to a pile of junk that would almost fit in a suitcase?

Many cars today also have air bags for additional protection. Porsche was the first manufacturer to introduce both driver and passenger air bags as standard in the United States on its 1990 models. But even if you have that additional built-in safety, *you must still wear the belts* for the car's safety features to be totally effective.

Like most racing drivers, I have had my share of accidents. The fact that I am still here to write this book today is in part due to having had my life saved by safety belts on more than one occasion.

On both the Czechoslovakian Rally with a Ford Cortina and the Monte Carlo Rally with a Porsche 911, I crashed head on into a tree (not the same one, of course) at about 60mph. In both cases

23

Talladega, 1993

In this series of photos, Neil Bonnett in car number 31, spins, is tapped in the side causing the car to lift and allow the air to get under it, then barrel rolls into the spectator safety fencing before coming to rest right side up in the infield grass where a dazed Bonnett is helped from the wreck...and immediately walks back, none the worse for wear to examine what's left! This crash hap-

pened at about 190mph. The fact that Neil walked away with just a couple of bruises is an outstanding testimony to NASCAR's safety rules. Note how the central part of the car, just like your road car, is virtually intact. The front and back have self-destructed, absorbing the energy along the way. Photos courtesy of Daytona International Speedway

24

my codriver and I were able to walk away with nothing more than sore necks and bruised shoulders from the effect of the seatbelts.

On another occasion, again in a Ford Cortina, I was practicing a hill climb at night in Luxembourg. I slid off the road at about 70mph and glanced off a tree, which flipped the car onto its roof. The car spun along upside down until it finally somersaulted off the edge of the road and slid backward down a steep slope, coming to rest against (yes, you guessed it) another solid tree. My codriver on that occasion was John Davenport who wore glasses. Although he lost them during the accident, when we came back the next morning to survey the wreckage, we even found his glasses undamaged underneath the car!

Perhaps most impressive of all was an accident in the German Grand Prix at the notorious and famous Nürburgring. Although I had a good position on the starting grid, I made a terrible start and both Mario Andretti in a Lotus and Jean-Pierre Beltoise in a Matra overtook me on the way to the first corner. Mario's car was an experimental one with Ferguson four-wheel-drive, and it had been so problematic during practice that he had never done a lap with a full fuel load. Halfway around the first lap the inevitable happened: The car bottomed out, and Mario lost control and slid off the road. Both left side wheels were ripped off and one of them came rolling and bouncing across the road. Beltoise just had room to squeeze between the wheel and the edge of the road, but by the time I arrived a few tenths of a second later it had made one more bound and closed the gap. My left front wheel hit it at about 120mph and I did a slow, lazy roll over the top of the bushes before crashing to the ground upside down in (of course) the trees. My right arm was almost torn off, my nose broken, and my face received a few cuts and bruises (this was in the days before full-face helmets), but six weeks later I was back in a race car!

Compare those results with my first ever car accident before the days of seatbelts. Driving my father's Wolseley 6/80, the car used by the British police at that time, a tire burst at about 70mph (we did not have such things as the superb speed-rated Goodyear Eagles in those days). The car launched itself into a series of end over ends before coming to rest on what was left of all four wheels. Having been bounced around like a ping pong ball in a washing machine, I found myself spread-eagled over the transmission tunnel in the rear of the car with a severe concussion and three broken vertebrae. The main structure of the car was relatively undamaged and had I been wearing seat belts I would probably have had little worse than a headache. As it was, I spent the next six months wearing a steel corset while my back healed!

If the macho look, or showing your friends how good you are is important, buckle up, you'll do a much better job of impressing them with your driving.

I can already hear the cries of "But what happens if I have an accident and land in a river, or an accident that causes the car to catch fire?" The answer to those or similar questions is simple. If you are wearing seatbelts and do have such an accident, you are *far more likely to be conscious* when the car stops and therefore capable of getting out than if you are *not* wearing belts!

In the midsixties (and still today) some of the world's leading rally drivers were from Finland. During practice for the Monte Carlo Rally in 1966, one of the famous flying Finns, Rauno Altonen, was driving a Mini Cooper S and crashed at high speed, at night, in the French mountains. Because it was a practice car, he did not have what was then the usual competition four-point harness, but only a three-point lap and diagonal. The car rolled a number of times and caught fire as it came to rest. Although Rauno was groggy, he was still conscious, and his codriver, Henry Liddon, was completely unhurt. By the time Henry had freed himself, the buckle of Rauno's seatbelt had welded itself together from the heat, but with the aid of some judicious wriggling they still had time to extricate him before he was burned!

Seatbelts are not a luxury, they should not be used on a whim, they should be treated as a necessity.

Seatbelts are not a luxury, they should not be used on a whim, they should be treated as a necessity. Whether you use a three-point, four-point, or full competition six-point harness, buckling up should be as fundamental as starting the engine. As long ago as the early sixties, those of us who drove in competition had already accepted seatbelts as a way of life. But even after they became mandatory in many countries, I still remember receiving rental cars in Italy with no seatbelts. Getting into an Italian rental car in those days I used to feel as naked as if I had gone out without my pants on!

Driving Clothing

Many things may influence what you wear when you are driving. If your business involves calling on half a dozen clients during an average day, it is obviously not practical to drive in casual clothes, rush into the rest room to change for every appointment, and change back again before heading for the next one! But try to keep your wardrobe to soft comfortable clothes. Take off your jacket and loosen your tie while you are driving—it will only take a moment or two to smarten up when you arrive for the next meeting. (Your jacket will look fresher too.)

Ladies, if you wear high-heeled shoes out of the car, keep a pair of comfortable flat-heeled ones in the car that you can easily slip on for driving.

Cotton, silk, and wool are comfortable materials that let the body breathe. Avoid nylon, polyester, or other synthetic textiles that tend to become uncomfortable when you sweat. (They can also melt and stick to you with disastrous results if you are unlucky enough to catch fire!) Actually, there is an old English saying that only horses sweat, gentlemen perspire, and ladies get uncomfortable. But you get my meaning.

When setting off on a leisure drive with no dress restrictions, ideally you should wear comfortable, loose-fitting clothes and a pair of soft, thin-soled shoes. Leather is probably best, and it is a good idea to keep a clean rag in the door pocket so that you can dry off the soles as you get in the car on a rainy day. Avoid rubber-soled shoes if possible, especially in the rain, as wet rubber on the rubber pedal covers will make for a very slippery contact and your feet are likely to slide off the pedals just when you don't need them to.

Although tennis shoes, running shoes, or whatever you call them are almost a uniform in terms of casual wear these days, they are usually not good to drive in because the soles are so thick that they allow little "feel" for the pedals. Plus, they are usually made of rubber.

I like to wear light leather-soled moccasins or, as an apparent contradiction to what I just said, soft, thin boating shoes. They do indeed have rubber soles, but they are nonslip rubber. And always make sure there is nothing lying around on the floor that might slide forward and interfere with your footwork. Nothing is more embarrassing than finding that the brake pedal won't work because your camera is wedged underneath it!

Sunglasses

A word about sunglasses. If you need to wear them, you might want to experiment with different brands or types, but in any case, beware of sunglasses that are more of a fashion statement than eye protection. Make sure that you can still really see when you are wearing them.

Years ago I was driving over a special stage in the Alpine Rally in France just as the sun was coming up. The bright sun in the pale blue sky made for a lot of glare and although I was wearing sunglasses, I found myself partly blinded going from sun to deep shade and back again. Three times in a few miles I misjudged distances and slid off the road. Nothing dramatic, just a few feet late in braking, but each time cost precious seconds as I had to reverse up before continuing. Finally, after the third time, I took my sunglasses off and threw them out the window—and have never worn sunglasses for driving since. I still wear them for sailing or flying, but only Polaroid, which seem to give the best antiglare protection while not affecting my depth perception.

Dress comfortably for everyday driving. This is my typical driving wear: lightweight cotton pants, light shirt, and soft, thin, non-slip boating shoes with no socks!

Chapter 2

Balance

The place: The French Alps
The time: 1968
The occasion: The 37th running of the Monte Carlo Rally

Just one year earlier I had led the Monte Carlo Rally in my Porsche 911S virtually all the way until the last special stage over the Col du Turini. To win Monte Carlo is every rally driver's dream

but victory had been snatched away from me at literally the eleventh hour by an unexpected blizzard that caught me with the wrong tires and allowed two other cars to overtake me and drop me back to third place.

This year, after three days spent driving from starting points all over Europe, followed by thirty-six hours of against-the-clock driving in the mountains, the leading sixty cars set out for what is es-

Monte Carlo Rally, 1968
Moments like this are worth all the hard work. Here co-driver David Stone and I display in front of the royal

family the silverware that our 1968 Monte Carlo Rally victory brought us. Robert de Hoé

Porsche 911, Monte Carlo Rally, 1968
The future victors at speed over the snow while a local gets a great close-up photo opportunity. Eric della Faille

sentially a 600km night race through the Maritime Alps above Monte Carlo and Nice.

Remembering the disappointment of a year ago I was finding it difficult to settle into a balanced rhythm. I had already been beaten—not by much, but beaten nevertheless, on the first two special stages by my own Porsche 911 teammate, Pauli Toivonen, as well as two of the French Renault Alpines. Now, on the long run to Saint Sauveur and the start of the third special stage, my codriver, David Stone, was lecturing me like a kindly old uncle. "You're trying too hard," he told me. "I'm being thrown around uncomfortably because you are thinking of speed rather than balancing the car the way you usually do.

"Forget about last year. Forget about the ice and snow. (We had spent the previous night going over the route checking the amounts of ice and snow on our corner-by-corner 'pace notes.') There might be less than last night, but not more. Forget it is Monte Carlo, just drive the way you normally do in the mountains, where you know you are the fastest—uphill and down!"

By the time we started the special stage over the Col de la Couillole he had gotten my nerves under control. As we waited for the starting signal, I was relaxed, comfortable, and felt that I could walk on air.

Tight and twisty on the way up but with long, fast stretches on the way down, the Couillole is a great test of both man and machine. It was a beautiful night with the moon reflecting eerily off the white snowbanks lining the seventeen-mile ribbon of asphalt. The road was mainly dry but still had some large patches of snow and ice in places, particularly on the descent. But we knew where they were and David would be able to give me plenty of warning as he read the road to me from the pace notes. With this in mind, we elected to go on racing tires and at the service point just before the start the mechanics had fitted a brand new set.

Ten minutes later we had crested the summit and were on the way down toward the village of Beuil. Reaching speeds of over 120mph, with our racing tires often slipping and sliding over the packed snow and ice before regaining grip on the

Porsche 911, Monte Carlo Rally, 1968
*Flat out down the Col de la Couillole. Could we have
taken two corners faster...or three?* Vic Elford collection

Porsche 911, Monte Carlo Rally, 1968
*On the way to winning the Monte Carlo Rally. Looks like
I had at least one ardent supporter on my side!* Vic
Elford collection

Porsche 911, Monte Carlo Rally, 1968
Same car, same "Monte," but this is at night over the Col du Turini. Note the lighting set-up; we'll talk more about it later. Eric della Faille

dry surface beyond, we used the pendulum effect of the 911's rear engine to help steer the car and were balanced as though on a tightrope. The slightest mistake and we would have fallen off. Car, tires, and above all, the crew, were absolutely at 100 percent, even using the snow banks as buffers as we sometimes exited corners too fast. But we made no mistakes, and our time of seventeen minutes was fifty-seven seconds quicker than the second car, more than enough to propel us to Porsche's first outright victory in the world's most famous and coveted rally.

Much later, when we had both recovered from the nervous exhaustion, David and I analyzed those seventeen minutes. He thought there were three corners that I could have taken quicker—I thought there were two!

Monte Carlo Rally, 1968
The spoils of victory at Monte Carlo, received from the late Princess Grace and Prince Rainier with a tiny Princess Stephanie appearing to hide behind mum's coat! Vic Elford collection

31

The Importance of Balance

Remember in the first chapter that the word *balance* was highlighted? This was for a very good reason: Balance is probably the *single most important* word in the art—and it is an art—of safe, controlled, high performance driving and will be emphasized throughout this book.

Have you ever tried walking on stilts? Balancing is difficult because your center of gravity is so high relative to the ground. Raising your center of gravity relative to that of the car has the same effect.

Balance is probably the single most important word in the art— and it is an art—of safe, controlled, high-performance driving.

Can you recall your first attempt at riding a bicycle? In my case, it was in a narrow alley behind a friend's house and every time the bike

Porsche 908, Nürburgring, 1968
Beautifully balanced, I "fly" the 908 Coupe toward the first of three victories I achieved for Porsche in the Nürburgring 1000km races. Werkfoto Porsche

32

leaned one way I leaned the other. Fortunately, the alley was narrow, with a high wooden fence on either side, so there was no room to fall off—but I did remove most of the skin from both elbows before finally getting the hang of it.

I have already talked about fitting yourself to the car or even fitting the car to you if necessary. Apart from the movement of the feet to control the pedals (notice I said just *the feet*, not the legs, which you will see later, should hardly move) and the hands and arms for the steering wheel and gearshift, the rest of the body should be tightly strapped in so that it feels like part of the car. A little leaning of the head toward the inside of a corner is acceptable—the way you lean in when you are riding on two wheels—but it should not be exaggerated.

Nürburgring, 1968
Savoring victory with co-driver Jo Siffert. Vic Elford collection

Porsche 911, Silverstone
Balance! Here with one wheel off the ground, I lead Paul Hawkins in his Lotus Cortina with two wheels in the air, in a British Touring Car (Sedan) Championship race at Silverstone. Maureen Magee

Porsche 908, Brands Hatch, 1969
No exaggerated head movement. Here I am going into the tight Druids Hairpin in a 908 during the 1969 Brands

Hatch 1000km race. I went on to finish second. Foto Kräling

Shuffle Steering and Balance

Remember in chapter 1 I discussed the positions of the hands on the steering wheel? One of the reasons this is so important is the effect it has on balance. Just for a moment try holding the steering wheel with both hands together at the top. Now, still holding the wheel with both hands like that, steer the car right and left (it might be wise to try this exercise in a deserted parking lot on Sunday morning where there is nothing to hit!). You will find it just doesn't feel right because by moving both arms together to the same side you create an asymmetrical situation.

Now go back to the 3 o'clock and 9 o'clock position and try it again. To start with, turn the wheel through 180 degrees; in other words, a full half turn. *Don't let go of the wheel*, just adjust your grip as the turn increases. Feels a lot better doesn't it? That's because all the elements of your body are now back in a symmetrical position.

Now let's go a stage further. Instead of just turning through 180 degrees (a half turn), keep going until you have turned the wheel through 270 degrees (three-quarters of a turn). "Wait a moment," I can hear you saying. "I would need arms like spaghetti to do that."

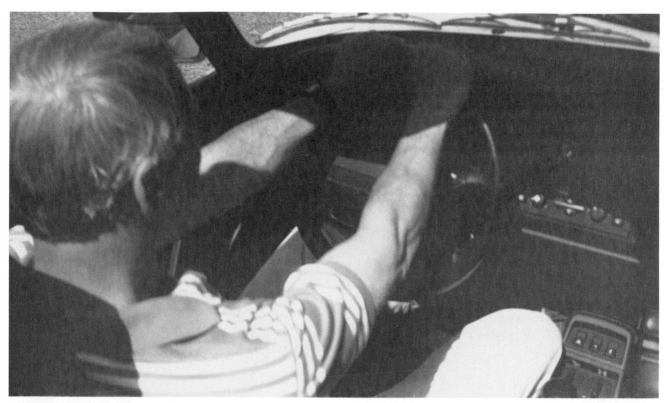

How not to hold the steering wheel.

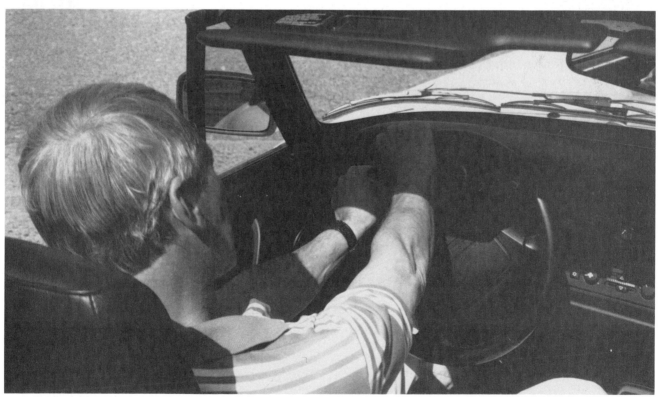

Feel how the body loses balance as the arms create an asymmetrical position?

It feels much better balanced like this, doesn't it?

Well, not exactly. The correct technique here is to keep the grip firm with the hand that is uppermost on the wheel (i.e., the left hand for a right turn, the right hand for a left turn) while relinquishing the grip with the lower hand when it has reached the half-turn position. Relinquish the grip *but leave the hand there* ready to regrip the wheel as it returns from its full turn position.

All Porsches have very direct steering, as do some other sports or sporty cars, and you will find that, with the exception of very tight turns in city traffic or the parking lot of your local supermarket where "shuffle steering" is more logical, mastering this technique will give you total *balanced* control of most driving situations.

Shuffle steering means just that: Shuffling the wheel from hand to hand but always keeping your left hand somewhere between the seven and eleven position and the right hand between the one and five position. For a left turn, for example, the right hand will take the wheel from the three position to the one position, whereupon the left hand will take it from the eleven position to the seven position. If you still need more turn, the right hand will take over at the five position and continue up to the one position, and so on. You will

use an even more evolved form of shuffle steering on snow, ice, gravel, or other loose surfaces, which I will discuss in a later chapter.

Weight Transfer

Driving does not mean just balancing left and right. It also means balancing up and down. Did you ever dive off a 10ft diving board and get your body balance wrong? Even if it does nothing more, it certainly leaves you with a sore back (or perhaps worse still, a sore front) for a few days.

For the moment, just notice what happens to your car, yourself, and your passengers as you drive. Each time you accelerate you are pushed back in the seat. You can see and feel that the car tends to lift up at the front and sit back on the rear wheels. Conversely, when you brake the nose dips and you are thrust forward against the seatbelts.

Driving does not mean just balancing left and right. It also means balancing up and down.

36

In fact, considerable weight transfer is taking place in both these circumstances. In acceleration, weight is taken off the front wheels and transferred to the rear, giving excellent traction for acceleration (in a rear-wheel-drive car) but less grip at the front wheels for steering. Under heavy braking, weight is transferred in the other direction, from the rear to the front. The harder you brake, the greater the weight transfer is. By the same token, the greater the weight transfer you can apply towards the front of the car, the harder you can brake without locking the front wheels.

Similarly, as you turn a corner to the left weight transfers from the left wheels to the right wheels. Again you can feel this weight transfer as your body and head tend to be pushed toward the outside of the corner.

These reactions are governed by the laws of physics. In a later chapter I will go into greater detail on how you can adjust the balance of the car, both left to right and fore and aft, as well as both at the same time, to steer it and even to lift it over obstacles in its path.

Spa-Francorchamps, 1971
At Eau Rouge, the first corner at the daunting Spa-Francorchamps circuit, just after the start of the 1000km rac in 1971. You can clearly see the effects of weight transfer. The number 1 Ferrari is heavily on the brakes in a straight line; number 22 Porsche 917 is still braking heavily but also getting sideways weight transfer as he turns into the corner; number 20 Porsche 917 has already released the brakes and the nose has come up as he begins to accelerate out of the corner. Eberhard Strähle

Chapter 3

Smoothness

The place: The city of Lyon, France
The time: 1967
The occasion: The Stuttgart/Lyon-Charbon-nières Rally

I had first driven a Porsche 911 on the Tour of Corsica Rally in 1966; in 1967 the rally cars were still prepared in the customer service department in Zuffenhausen under the direction of my great friends Huschke von Hanstein and engineer Hermann Briem. Until now, all of Porsche's competition effort had been directed toward circuit racing, but a third place in Corsica followed by another third, after leading for so long, on the Monte Carlo Rally, had opened their eyes to the benefits to be gained by rally successes.

Huschke and Hermann paid me the compliment of absolute trust in everything concerned with the rally program, even to designing the specification of the car.

Porsche was one of the first manufacturers to use a five-speed gearbox in its production cars and at the same time also offered a vast range of alternative gearbox and final-drive ratios. This gave us a tremendous advantage over other manufacturers who could usually change only the final-drive ratios but not those in the gearbox. Later this year I would win the Tulip Rally with a Porsche 911, whose top speed at 7200rpm in fifth gear was only 100mph but which, with five equally spaced gears, gave shatteringly fast acceleration!

For the Stuttgart/Lyon-Charbonnières Rally we calculated that the Stuttgart Solitude race would account for about 40 percent of the total test time, so we had to balance the requirements of the racetrack and its 140mph plus top speed with those of the hill climbs to come later.

Normally on a Porsche 911 designed to go quickly in the mountains, first gear is used only for starting. Once under way the car is driven as if it has a four-speed transmission, using second, third, fourth, and fifth gears. In this case we would have to reverse the process, using first, second, third, and fourth for the mountains. Fifth would be so high that it could only be used on the racetrack.

But that meant using a first gear at least as high as our normal second. I would have to be very, very careful getting it away from the start line on all the uphill mountain climbs.

The rally had started three days earlier in Porsche's hometown of Stuttgart where the first competitive test had been the race on the high-speed Stuttgart Solitude racetrack.

Now it was midnight. Cold, dark, and raining. We had won the race at Solitude and with my "back-to-front" gearbox had continued to build an unassailable lead. All the competition driving was behind us and we had only to traverse Lyon and reach the casino town of Charbonnières to record our first win in a Porsche 911.

Suddenly the needle on the rev counter was mounting—but not the one on the speedometer! Despite all the babying of the car off the start lines on the hill climbs, the clutch was worn out and starting to slip.

I was faced with the longest thirty minutes of *smooth* driving of my life. Instead of mashing the throttle pedal to the floor after each red light, I had to caress it as though there were a fresh egg between it and my foot. Fortunately, few natives of the city of Lyon are on the road at midnight. Not for nothing is Lyon known as the gastronomic capital of the world, and those who had partaken of its hospitality were home by now savoring a last Cognac before bedtime—unless they were motor racing fans, in which case they were waiting with baited breath at the casino of Charbonnières for the winners of the rally to arrive!

In many European countries, roads are subject to "the priority of the right," which means that at junctions where no right of way is established by a

Porsche 911, Stuttgart-Lyon-Charbonnières, 1967
The car had to be pushed into position for the photos.
Read on and you'll see why! Jean Sejnost

"Stop" or "Yield" sign, the vehicle approaching from the right has priority. Just one more obstacle in our path as I tiptoed my way across the third largest city in France with a car that I knew, if it stopped once, would never start again. With my co-driver David Stone peering left and right at all the intersections, trying to calculate, gauge, or just simply guess the traffic light sequences, we made

it to the finish line at Charbonnières and victory. And being France, the French champagne tasted great!

When the mechanics went to move the car from the impound area the next morning they had to push it. Despite having cooled down during the night, there was no clutch left at all. It was undrivable!

Porsche 911, Stuttgart-Lyon-Charbonnières, 1967
Forty percent of the total test time on the Lyon-Charbon- *nières Rally was on the Solitude Ring racetrack.* Werkfoto Porsche

The Importance of Smoothness

If *balance* is the single most important word in driving, *smoothness* is a close second.

Next time you have the opportunity, watch how a good truck driver can wheel a monster eighteen-wheeler around without sudden braking or acceleration, without sudden changes of direction. If they can do it, surely you can too in a vehicle that is only a fraction of the size and weight and a lot better balanced.

If balance is the single most important word in driving, smoothness is a close second.

Anticipation

One more little ingredient to add to create that flowing smoothness is *anticipation*. Don't stare fixedly at the tailgate of the pickup a few car lengths in front of you. Be aware of what is happening all around you: to the sides, using your peripheral vision; to the rear, using your mirrors; and especially way ahead in front of you. Try to look through the windows of the car in front to see what is happening down the road. If that is not possible, drop back a little so that you can see past one side or the other, particularly if the road bends a little.

It may get you a few strange looks from other drivers, but a good way to exercise your anticipation and awareness of what is going on around you is to give a spoken running commentary as you drive. Talk to yourself about everything that you see: A ball running out into the road probably means a child is going to be following it; a small pair of feet and legs beneath a parked car can warn of an unexpected dash into the road in front of you. On a rural road or freeway, notice the condition of the road shoulders. If the road was suddenly blocked in front of you, could you safely drive off the road to avoid an accident?

To drive smoothly you must anticipate.

You will be amazed to find that with a little practice, you will become so aware of things you never noticed before that even at 30mph there is not time to say it all!

I'm sure that many of you reading this book fly or ride in private airplanes. At first, listening to

Porsche 911, Stuttgart-Lyon-Charbonnières, 1967
The background shows a typical mountain road as used in European rallies. This one is high in the French Alps as navigator David Stone and I piloted our 911 toward our Lyon-Charbonnières victory. Vic Elford collection

air traffic controllers probably sounded like listening to a foreign language. But after a while, you could understand what was being said, even above the crackle and static of the airwaves, because with experience *you had already anticipated and knew* what the instructions or message were *likely* to be.

Smooth Transitions

In a car, knowing what you are probably going to need to do helps you to do it right when the time comes. Watching motor racing from the in-car TV camera gives a good insight to the way drivers anticipate. You will notice that they often act and react extremely quickly, but they are rarely in a

Porsche 911, Stuttgart-Lyon-Charbonnières, 1967
*Smoothness was the key to climbing the Freiberg hill
climb on the Lyon-Charbonnières. I was doing a great deal
of the steering with the throttle and the balance of the car
rather than with the steering wheel.* Julius Weitmann

hurry, because whenever they have to do something they have usually anticipated doing it well in advance. All the movements flow together to form one continuous transition. Even though with practice you will be able to go from full throttle to maximum braking in only hundredths of a second, it must be done *smoothly*. Turning from a straight must be a *smooth* flowing transition into and then out of the corner.

Stamping on the gas or the brake pedal or jerking the steering wheel will upset that delicate balance I discussed in the previous chapter.

My first ever international rally as a driver was the RAC Rally of Great Britain in 1961. John Sprinzel was a well-known English driver who had also established a solid reputation for making Austin A35s and Austin-Healey "Bug Eye" Sprites go indecently quickly. He had prepared his own car for the rally when at the last minute he was offered a drive in a factory, or "works" car. Since his car was ready, it seemed a shame not to use it, so he offered it to two penniless, determined, would-be future world champions: Paul Hawkins and me.

Paul was one of the most colorful characters ever to leave his native Australia to seek fame and fortune on the European racing scene. Son of a lay preacher, his face looked as though it had been carved out of a piece of granite—with a blunt chisel. At a Silverstone race where Paul drove a new Lotus Cortina and I was in a Porsche 911 *(see photo page 33)*, we were parked side by side in the paddock and when, after the race, Colin Chapman asked his opinion of the car, Paul was able to spend two minutes telling him, without ever repeating the same swear word once!

Paul had never done a rally in his life, and when we met at John's workshop he announced that he could not drive at night and did not know the top of a map from the bottom. So I would have to navigate during the day while he drove—then drive *and* navigate at night while he slept!

I have always had plenty of endurance, so the first part of the ultimatum wasn't too bad. As far as the second part goes, for those of you who have ever experienced the inside of an Austin-Healey Sprite, I suppose I must have driven pretty smoothly because Paul really did sleep at night!

Sadly, Paul was one of many who lost his life a few years later in a racing crash, before track owners and organizers realized that race cars and trees just a few feet from the track edge do not belong together.

In normal road driving or on a racetrack, the car should always be driven as though it were on rails. It may look and feel spectacular when the car is sideways but modern chassis, suspension, and tires give the best results when the car stays glued to the road. The exceptions to this rule are when driving on ice and snow or other loose surfaces, and I will discuss them later. But whatever the conditions, even on loose surfaces where you are steering the car with the throttle, you must still be *smooth*.

Chapter 4

The Cars

**The place: The Mulsanne Straight, Le Mans.
The time: 4:02 P.M., one Saturday in June 1970.
The occasion: 24 Hours of Le Mans. First lap.**

I was heading down the Mulsanne Straight at over 240mph in the fastest racing car ever built, the only 5.0-liter, long-tailed Porsche 917 entered in this year's race.

Porsche 917, Le Mans, 1970
Here I was in the long-tail 917, number 25. Jo Siffert in number 20 has just beaten me away from the start. By the end of the Mulsanne straight on the first lap I had al-ready made good use of the 25mph speed differential between the long-tail car and the others and was leading a gaggle of Porsche 917s and Ferrari 512s by more than 50 yards. Werkfoto Porsche

Porsche 906, Le Mans, 1967
My first time at the 24 Hours of Le Mans driving a Porsche 906 in 1967 was also my first victory: fifth over-all and winner of what was then the Group 5 Sports Car class. Maximum speed on the Mulsanne straight, about 175mph. Dave Friedman

Porsche 917, Le Mans, 1969
My first time in the first Porsche 917 at Le Mans in 1969. Maximum speed on the Mulsanne straight, about 225mph, some 35mph faster than anything else in the race. A broken oil seal put co-driver Richard Attwood and I out of the race with only three hours left when we were leading by more than 50 miles! Vic Elford collection

Porsche 917, Le Mans, 1970
My long-tail in action in 1970. The only 5.0-liter long-tail in the race, its maximum speed on the Mulsanne straight was almost 245mph! Werkfoto Porsche

Porsche 917, Le Mans, 1970
The car and I featured in the Steve McQueen movie Le
Mans. *Werkfoto Porsche*

Although I had been on the pole position, which I had won after setting a new lap record and being the first person ever to lap the 8.4-mile circuit at over 150mph two days earlier, Jo Siffert had just beaten me away at the start. I was sandwiched between Jo and Pedro Rodriguez in the two Gulf-Wyer 917s, as we had streamed under the Dunlop bridge, down through the 'esses,' and around Tertre Rouge.

Now at maximum speed the smooth, slippery shape of the long-tail had taken over. Past the two Hunaudières restaurants huddled together on the left of the road, where customers sipping their first cocktail of the evening, only 3ft from the edge of the road, see little more than a white flash as the car goes by, covering the ground at more than 350ft a second!

I go through the Mulsanne Kink, which I take flat out in a long, smooth, balanced arc and on toward the notorious Mulsanne Corner. About 500 yards from the corner I feel the front of the car get light as it crests the famous hump; the wheels do not quite leave the ground but there is so little weight on the front ones that the steering has little effect.

As the weight settles again onto all four wheels I glance in the mirror and see that the colossal speed advantage the long-tail body gave me on the more than three-mile straight, over half of which is covered at sustained maximum speed, has opened up a big gap to the pursuing cars. Even just a quick glance shows Jo and Pedro being hounded by four Ferrari 512s.

No matter what car you are driving, there is only one speed for the Mulsanne Corner, about 40mph. Past the 300-yard marker board I go

Porsche 917, Le Mans, 1971
A "photographer's eye" view of the beautiful sweeping curves of the Martini Racing Team long-tail 917 at Le Mans in 1971. Vic Elford collection

Ferry Porsche, Porsche 908, 1968
Dr. Ferry Porsche with his latest model in 1968, the 908 Coupe. Only two of these cars were ever built: Jo Siffert

and I won the Nürburgring 1000km in one in 1968. Werkfoto Porsche smoothly, firmly, then harder and harder onto the brakes. In less than 300 yards the speed comes down from over 240mph to about 40mph. Even in daylight, those standing at the edge of the track at this point can see the brake discs glowing white hot through the wheels. Balancing the car delicately through the Mulsanne Corner (the long-tail doesn't take kindly to being jerked around, even in slow corners) I accelerate cleanly and smoothly for the next two miles until I brake again from 200mph for Indianapolis Corner.

Through the right-hand kink before Indianapolis, just a lift from the gas pedal leaves the car poorly positioned for the corner but has the advantage of keeping the high speed going longer. I take the short straight and then the very slow, narrow, right-hand Arnage Corner in first gear. Then back up through the gears to over 200mph in fifth before, with a little touch on the brakes to steady the car, I change down to fourth while the car is airborne over the little humpback bridge. I instantly flick right toward the famous and notorious left-hand White House Corner, and then I accelerate hard again to the left and right of the Ford Chicane to swoop back onto the pit straight alone. There can be few experiences in the world as exhilarating as those first 3 1/2 minutes at Le Mans in a car like the long-tail 917!

Ferdinand Piëch
A youthful Ferdinand Piëch, who had a profound influence on Porsche racing success in the sixties and early seventies. Werkfoto Porsche

Ferry and Ferdinand Porsche, Porsche 356, 1948
Dr. Ferdinand "Ferry" Porsche with his father Professor Ferdinand Porsche and the first car to bear the famous

name. Known as the Typ 356, it was built in a shed in the town of Gmünd, Austria, in 1948. Werkfoto Porsche

Porsche Cars

Dr. Ferdinand Porsche built the first car to bear his name for himself because he simply could not find what he wanted in the market. His genius and dedication were inherited by his nephew Dr. Ferdinand Piëch who will probably go down in history as one of the greatest automobile engineers of all time.

From the 911, which first saw the light of day twenty-eight years ago (and is still the standard by which other sports cars are measured) to the unbelievably lightweight 908 and perhaps the greatest racing car of all time, the fabulous 917 in all its variations, all were the products of Ferdinand Piëch's fertile imagination. He left Porsche in 1972 and subsequently became chairman of Audi, where he was responsible for a range of passenger cars second to none, as well as the sensational World Rally Champion Quattro Coupe. At the time of writing, he had recently been appointed to the chairmanship of the Volkswagen group.

Porsche Handling Traits

Before we start talking about the cars and their different handling characteristics, there are some phenomena that you need to be familiar with. Don't worry, I am not going to blind you with science, I'll just give you some very simple definitions. I will go into a more technical analysis of why these things happen and what to do about them in a later chapter.

Understeer

Also described as "pushing" or "plowing," understeering occurs when you turn the car into a corner and it still has a tendency to go straight on.

Porsche Typ 911 Debut, 1963
A proud Ferry Porsche perches on the fender of a 904 while he surveys the first 911. The 911 was originally known as project 901. The name had to be changed as Peugeot had registered the sole right to use three figure numbers with a "0" in the middle to designate road car model names. Werkfoto Porsche

Porsche Typ 911 Debut, 1963
The first Porsche 911. Werkfoto Porsche

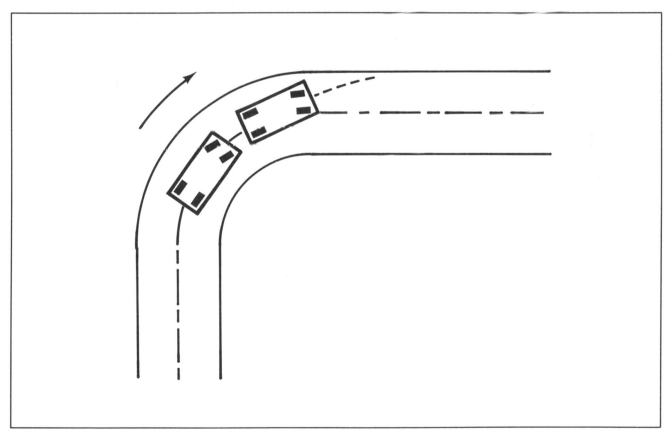

With understeer, even though the front wheels are turned hard into the corner, the car will not follow the ideal line but "pushes" out on the wider line.

You find yourself winding on more and more steering to follow the desired arc through the corner. This will occur with any car, even a Porsche, if it is still in the process of slowing down as you turn the wheel to steer into a corner.

Oversteer

Also described as "loose," oversteering is the opposite of understeering. Having turned into a corner, the car turns more sharply than desired and the rear tends to lose grip and slide outward. Oversteer can be provoked, both intentionally and unintentionally. With smooth application of power in a corner, the Porsche 968 or 928 can be pushed into a controllable oversteering mode and literally steered with the throttle.

The 911 has a tendency to oversteer and is particularly susceptible to throttle changes in a corner.

Neutral Balance

Providing you make no excessive acceleration or braking demands on the car, it will neither understeer nor oversteer but will follow a "neutral" balanced line around a corner.

While all of these conditions are largely dependent on the design of the car (its weight distribu-

tion, spring rates, and other built-in properties) they can be affected by the input from the driver.

Front-Wheel Drive

In looking at the basic handling characteristics of different cars, let us start with the only one *not* made by Porsche.

Front-wheel-drive cars exist for three fundamental reasons. First, because the entire power and drivetrain package are all together at the front in one unit, they are cheaper to build. Second, with no transmission tunnel or driven rear axle taking up room, they allow more useable space within the vehicle. Third, in the hands of many everyday drivers whose only notion of driving is that you push one pedal to go, the other one to stop, and you turn the steering wheel to point the car in roughly the right direction, they are inherently safe.

The front engine and power train configuration means that front-wheel-drive cars have a weight bias toward the front. Indeed, depending on the make and model, the weight distribution may be as high as 60 percent over the front wheels and as little as 40 percent at the rear.

In production form, they all understeer. The inexperienced driver arriving too fast into a corner

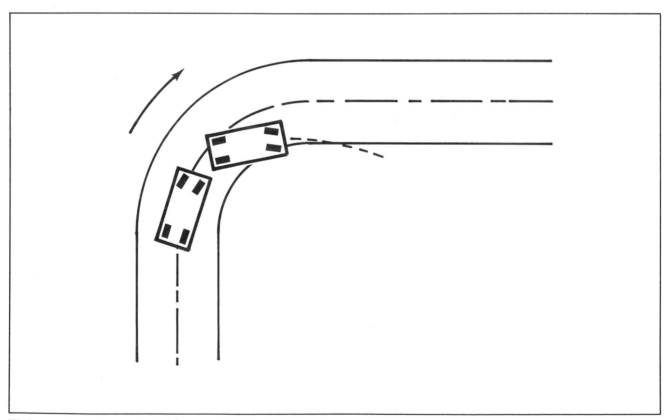

With oversteer, the car turns sharper than desired and takes a tighter line.

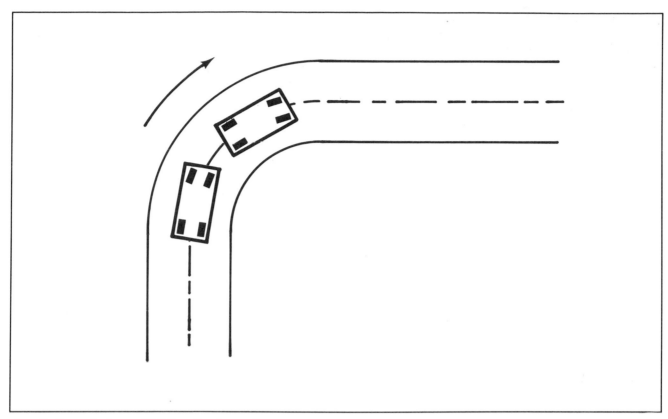

A perfectly neutral car will follow the chosen line.

will usually have a natural reflex action—lift off the throttle pedal. With a front-wheel-drive car that is the correct thing to do. It cuts off the transmission of power to the road (which was using up some of the capability of the front tires). At the same time it transfers more weight to the front wheels, which in turn gives them added grip to turn the car.

I like to use the term "negative safety" concerning front-wheel-drive cars; in these cars, doing nothing, or at best having almost a panic reflex action, is, in fact, the safest thing to do.

In the heyday of the Mini Cooper, which had so much weight over the front wheels that a really strong person could lift the back of the car off the ground singlehanded, we used to joke that the only reason it had rear wheels was to stop the body from dragging on the ground!

I like to use the term "negative safety" concerning front-wheel-drive cars. In cars with front-wheel drive, doing nothing, or at best having almost a panic reflex action, is, in fact, the safest thing to do. There are some "positive" things that can be done with front-wheel drive and I will discuss them later on.

Rear-Wheel Drive: Front Engine, Front Transmission

Engine and gearbox coupled together at the front and just the rear axle providing power transmission to the road has been the traditional layout for decades. Still nose heavy, like the front-wheel-drive cars, it is basically an understeering configuration. However, because of the comparatively light loading on the rear wheels, it can be tricky to drive under extreme conditions.

Rear-Wheel Drive: Front Engine, Rear Transmission

As long ago as the midseventies, Porsche pioneered the splitting of the engine and transmission in sports cars in order to create almost equal weight distribution on both front and rear wheels. This is the layout of the Porsche 944, 968, and 928, and the result is an almost perfectly balanced vehicle.

Porsche 968
The beautifully balanced 968 Coupe. Affordable luxury and performance today. Werkfoto Porsche/Dick Kelley

It is vital to cultivate a sense of balance and develop the smoothness if you want to get the best out of the 911.

The engine is at the front and a combined gearbox and rear axle, called a transaxle, is at the rear. Not only does this provide almost perfect fifty-fifty weight distribution, it also provides a very high polar moment of inertia, which endows the car with great stability at high speed, especially in the event of crosswinds. It also means that the car remains almost neutral in its handling and its ultimate comportment can be greatly influenced by the input from a skillful driver.

Rear-Wheel Drive: Midengine

For the Porsche fan, midengine means a 914. Once again, Porsche was a pioneer in midengined sports cars, but there are others. Ferrari's Testarossa and Toyota's MR2 are two current midengined cars, and in the early seventies there

was a successful midengined rally car from Italy, the Lancia Stratos. The main difference between the Lancia Stratos and the others mentioned above, is that the Lancia was conceived and designed to be a rally winner first—then adapted to become a street-legal vehicle afterward, whereas the Porsche 914, as well as the others, were originally designed and built as road-going sports cars and then modified for competition afterward.

Like the 944, 968, or 928, the 914 also has approximately fifty-fifty weight distribution, but in-

The 911 is perhaps the most maligned car ever built. The stories usually come from people who assume that because of their rear weight bias, 911s automatically spin the moment conditions are anything but ideal.

stead of the weight being concentrated in two masses, one at each end, it is all concentrated in the middle. Like the 944, 968, or 928, this makes for a well-balanced, neutral handling car. However, as opposed to the others, it has a very low polar moment of inertia, which has two significant effects on its handling. It tends to be susceptible to crosswinds, and on slippery surfaces it rotates extremely quickly.

With the high polar moment of inertia of the 944, 968, and 928 cars, the sizable mass at each end must be moved in order to make the car rotate, hence its great stability. However, the 914, not having this mass at each end, reacts more quickly to steering and throttle input and is rather more "nervous" to drive.

Rear-Wheel Drive: Rear Engine

The 911 is perhaps the most maligned car ever built. Anytime car enthusiasts get together they tell horrendous stories of 911s spinning or leaving the road backward. Any black marks on the guard rail around freeway exits are automatically attributed to out-of-control 911s.

Curiously, few, if any, of these stories are recounted by 911 drivers themselves. They usually come from people who assume that because of their rear weight bias, 911s automatically spin the moment conditions are anything but ideal.

The truth of the matter is that although early 911s were a little more difficult to drive than "conventional" cars, largely because they had comparatively narrow wheels and tires, once you master the technique, you can do things with a 911 that, if not impossible, are certainly much more difficult with other cars. However, it is vital to cultivate the sense of balance and develop the smoothness discussed earlier if you want to get the best out of this car.

The weight bias of a Porsche 911 is roughly the opposite of that of a front-wheel-drive car with approximately 40 percent on the front wheels and 60 percent on the rear wheels.

All-Wheel Drive

There is one more type of car that we have not yet looked at and that is four-wheel drive, or all-wheel drive as it is sometimes called. Depending on where the weight distribution is, it will handle basically as shown above for its two-wheel-drive counterpart.

In other words, the fundamental handling and balance of a Porsche Carrera 4 will resemble that of a 911 or Carrera 2. Similarly, an Audi Quattro will be like a front engine/front transmission, rear-wheel drive. But there are many subtle differences in the way they must be driven to get the best out of them, and I will examine some of those subtleties in a later chapter.

Handling and Pivot Points

In order to better understand the behavior of each type of car, let's look at where the various "pivot" points are with the aid of the following diagrams. By "pivot" point, I mean the imaginary point around which the car will rotate when cornering or sliding.

In the case of front-wheel drive, you will see that there really is not a pivot point. Everything is more or less centered over the front wheels: They lead and the rest follows.

For a conventional front engine, rear-wheel drive, the pivot point is perhaps a third of the way back from the front wheels. Having a good proportion of the engine/transmission mass very close to the pivot point means that this type of car is very stable, but at very high speeds or on slippery surfaces, the light loading over the rear wheels allows them to rotate very quickly.

In a front engine/rear transaxle car the pivot point is right in the middle, but the mass at each end makes the rotation very predictable and controllable.

With a midengine car, the pivot point is again right in the middle, but the lack of weight at each end means that it can rotate very quickly.

Finally, the rear-engine car, which today means quite simply the 911, has its pivot point more or less on the center line of the front wheels. So much weight at the rear causes a pendulum effect as the car rotates and can create problems for inexperienced drivers. As there is so much mass to get moving, it starts off almost imperceptibly and slowly builds up as the momentum increases. Drivers who get into trouble with a 911 usually do so because they have not developed a sufficient sense of *balance* and *feel* for what is happening. That first moment when the pendulum starts to swing goes unnoticed and by the time the driver realizes it is under way it has accelerated to such a point that it is too late to control it.

Now you can see the need for balance and smoothness. The instant the rear of a 911 starts to move it must be controlled. During over twenty years of teaching high-performance driving, I have noticed that virtually every single person I have taught—even those who have had some competition experience—start with one basic fault. They do not move quickly enough. In many cases they are simply unaware that the car will accept rapid steering or other inputs. Often it is because they simply are not sufficiently "at one" with the car to feel its balance and are afraid that a rapid movement will upset the equilibrium.

Wrong.

Remember how you thrilled to the high-wire tightrope walkers at the circus when you were a child? As they walked across the wire, they did not wait until they were leaning over at a 30-degree

DKW, Tulip Rally, 1962
Note all the weight over the front wheels. Vic Elford collection

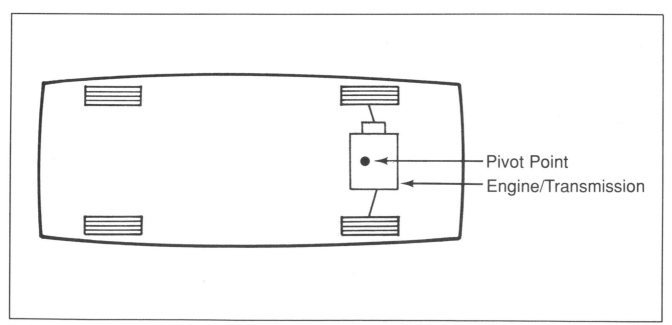

Pivot Point
Engine/Transmission

With front-wheel drive, most of the weight is centered over the front wheels—including the pivot point.

angle before trying to come back upright. They were in constant *rapid* movement, staying in an almost vertical position the whole time. Although, as I said earlier, you must never be in a hurry when driving a car, there are times when you *must* move quickly. The car must always be in a constant state of balance, not a succession of out of balance sequences joined together by desperate recovery measures.

DKW, Tulip Rally, 1962
Classic front-wheel-drive of the early sixties: my 750cc DKW. Vic Elford collection

Lotus Cortina, British RAC Rally, 1966
Here I am at speed in the Lotus Cortina on the RAC Rally of Great Britain. The Lotus Cortina was one of the best traditional front-engine, rear-wheel-drive cars ever. Foster and Skeffington Ltd.

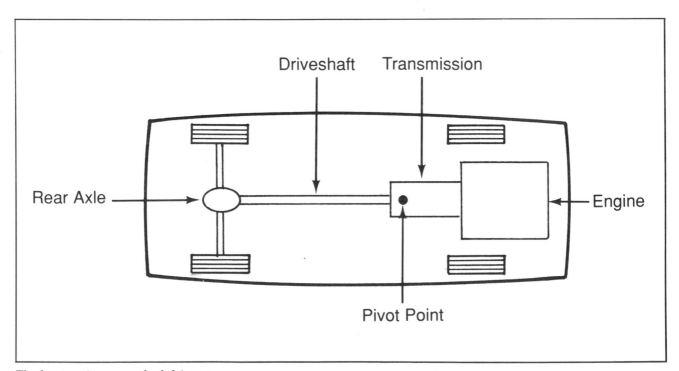

The front-engine, rear-wheel-drive setup.

Porsche 928
The Porsche 928, which pioneered the front-engine, rear-transaxle configuration for sports cars. Werkfoto Porsche/Dick Kelley

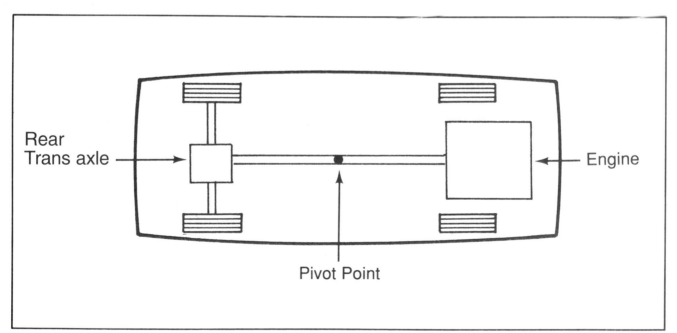

Rear
Trans axle

Engine

Pivot Point

The front-engine, rear-transaxle setup gives almost a fifty-fifty weight distribution.

Porsche 914
The 914 was a classic midengine sports car. Werkfoto
Porsche

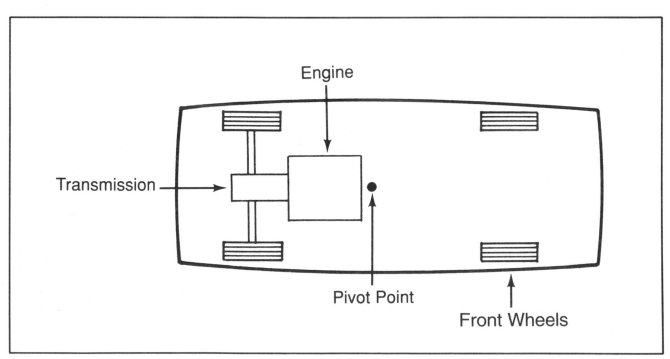

A midengine layout gives almost a fifty-fifty weight distribution, but lack of weight at each end makes for "nervous" handling.

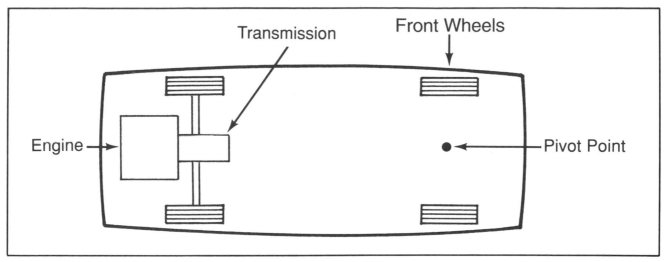

A rear-engined car such as a 911 features a pivot point that is separated from the weight concentration.

Porsche 911T, British RAC Rally, 1967
My 911T at speed on the British RAC Rally in 1967. Vic Elford collection

Porsche 911 RS America
The 1992 RS America that I was largely responsible for while working for Porsche Cars North America. Out-wardly little has changed on the 911 in more than twenty-five years. Underneath the bodywork, it's a different story. Werkfoto Porsche/Dick Kelley

Chapter 5

The Equipment

The place: Corsica
The time: 1966
The occasion: Le Tour de Corse (Tour of Corsica)

In 1966, the Renault Alpine 110 had replaced the Renault 8 Gordini as the car of choice for the French contingent. Both were tiny by today's

American standards and like the Porsche 911, both were true rear-engined cars, which endowed them with exceptional maneuverability on the incredibly narrow, twisting, mountain roads of Corsica.

Known as the rally of 10,000 corners, the Tour of Corsica had always been the exclusive domain of French drivers. With their driving skills developed

Porsche 911S, Corsica Rally, 1966
Ready for my first ever start in a Porsche, the 1966 Tour de Corse with a 911S. Although using the rally as a learning experience in driving the 911, I finished a mag-
nificent third—causing Porsche to re-think its approach to rallying and cementing my relationship with the marque that was to last until this day. Vic Elford collection

Porsche 911S, Corsica Rally, 1966
"Porsches don't break"—even in the beautiful but legendarily rugged mountains of Corsica. Vic Elford collection

and honed in the Alps they had been virtually alone in the yearly quest for victory in Corsica.

But during my three bittersweet years driving for Ford, I had already dispelled the myth that only the Scandinavians could drive on ice and snow and that only the French could drive in the mountains.

So why not Corsica as well?

Since my first visit to France many years earlier, I had discovered a real affinity with the country and the people. So the opportunity of spending an extra week there, tackling one of the most driver-intensive rallies in the world, was one not to be missed.

In 1965, I had taken my own rally-prepared Ford Anglia to Corsica just to look. What a rally! I retired after about six hours of the twenty-four-hour event with oil-pressure problems but I was more determined than ever to return with a car capable of winning.

I had first met Porsche competition director Baron Fritz Huschke von Hanstein some four months earlier after yet another disappointing and frustrating event in a Ford, the Alpine Rally. The Porsche 911 had started to make a tentative entry

onto the European rally scene and I had been seduced by its looks, its specification, and what I believed to be its winning potential.

Although Porsche did not really have a rally program, Huschke agreed to lend me a 911 for Corsica in 1966. No practice car (I would have to use a rental car), no money (I would have to pay my own personal expenses), and only one van with two mechanics to provide service for me and Gunter Klass in a second car.

My codriver David Stone and I had done a very serious reconnaissance in a rented Simca Aronde after which we met up with Huschke and the mechanics as they arrived with the rally cars on the quayside at Ajaccio. We opened up the van and looked inside to find only wheels and tires. I asked Huschke when the spare parts would be arriving, and he replied, "But there are no spare parts. Porsches don't break."

After all the ups and downs of my three tumultuous years with Ford, he had to be joking!

"Come on Huschke, there has to be something that breaks, even on a Porsche. I'm part of the team now; you can tell me, so when something breaks at least I'll know what it might be."

"No, my boy," was the response, "you don't understand. Porsches, even rally-prepared Porsches, simply don't break."

I had already decided that this would be an event with no dramatics but would serve as my apprenticeship in learning to drive a 911. Driving comfortably and smoothly, well within my limits, I still finished third, behind two of the incredible little Alpines, driven by two Frenchmen, of course. Just as important, I brought the car home without a scratch.

The following year, 1967, we went back again and were second going into the last special stage. The night had been long, wet, and foggy, and with Huschke's permission we threw caution to the winds in the effort to take first place. The road was drying a little, which we thought would favor the Porsche over the leading Lancia Fulvia of Sandro Munari, and I made no secret of our intentions, hoping to force him into a mistake. Unfortunately, it was I who made the mistake, hitting a wet patch and spinning off into the trees (of course) at high speed. By the time I got the car back on the road, not only was Munari out of danger, but my own Porsche teammate Pauli Toivonen had also passed me. Once again we had to settle for third place.

I asked Huschke when the spare parts would be arriving, and he replied, "But there are no spare parts. Porsches don't break."

But Huschke was right. Even under these exacting conditions, nothing broke!

The next year, 1968, we were back again. Having proved beyond any doubt that we were strong contenders against the French in a 911S, this year we were strong favorites, driving a 911R prototype with an experimental 2.0-liter, twin-cam engine. The engine, which I drove here and on the Cevennes Rally a couple of weeks later but which never saw the light of day in a production car, was an absolute marvel, with power and torque from 3000rpm all the way to an incredible 8200rpm.

But driving what we were sure was an unbeatable car, we were out within 15 kilometers of the start, with what was strongly and generally suspected to be a case of sabotage, when the oil filter simply unscrewed itself, draining all the engine oil out of the system.

Perhaps the most incredible part of this story is that not only in Corsica, but everywhere else as well—from the rigors of Monte Carlo to the cold of Sweden in winter; from the demanding Nürbur-

gring racetrack to an entire season of race winning in England—Huschke was right. No production-based 911 that I drove, *ever* broke—anything!

Porsche Engines

How does the car work?

First perhaps, is the engine.

In a Porsche 968, that means the largest, most powerful normally aspirated four-cylinder engine ever made with 236hp and 225lb-ft of torque. Thanks to its double counterrotating balance shafts, it is also perhaps the smoothest four-cylinder engine ever made.

The Porsche 928 has a magnificent 5.4-liter V-8 engine, producing no less than 345hp and a massive 369lb-ft of torque. All this with double-knock sensors and advanced electronic management giving almost turbinelike smoothness.

My favorite car of all time (I'm sure you've guessed by now), the Porsche 911 (now known as the Carrera 2 or Carrera 4), has a 3.6-liter, horizontally opposed six-cylinder engine, giving 247hp and 228lb-ft of torque.

Porsche Transmissions

Power is transmitted to the road by a variety of transmissions, depending on the model.

The 968 has the choice of a superb close-ratio six-speed manual gearbox or the remarkable Porsche/Bosch/ZF developed, Tiptronic dual-function automatic.

The 928 has a conventional five-speed or an advanced four-speed automatic.

For the current 911 versions, there is also a five-speed for both two-wheel- and four-wheel-drive versions, with the addition of Tiptronic for the two-wheel-drive cars.

If you do not drive a Porsche, your car may have a four-, five-, six-, eight-, ten-, or even twelve-cylinder engine and power will be transmitted by one of the above transmissions. (Though not the Tiptronic, which is still a Porsche exclusive.)

Porsche Suspension

Suspension usually consists of one spring for each wheel, one shock absorber for each wheel, and one antisway bar (also known as an antiroll bar) front and rear.

Advanced technology in modern racing is rapidly changing the conception of suspension systems and features many advances that will undoubtedly find their way into road cars of the future. Since space and weight are vital factors in the design of a race car, many now use one single spring/shock absorber unit that controls both front wheels or both rear wheels.

Even more exotic is the technology in some Formula 1 cars, where there are *no* springs *or* shock absorbers! The entire suspension is operated by computer-controlled hydraulic pumps at each wheel. One of the enormous advantages of such a system is that with the computer making thousands of adjustments per second, the ride height is maintained absolutely at constant preset limits. With aerodynamics playing such a crucial role in the performance of these cars, such a suspension can provide a big advantage over the competition.

But back to the real world.

The springs serve to absorb unevenness of the road surface, partly for reasons of comfort and partly to maintain the balance of the car. The "spring rate," which is the amount of force that must be exerted on the spring to compress it a given distance, depends on the weight carried by each individual wheel, thus controlling the balance of the car. Adjustment of the spring rate can also be used to change the understeer or oversteer characteristics of the car.

The shock absorbers do not really absorb shocks at all. What they do is *dampen* the wheel movement when it compresses and decompresses the spring. For this reason they are often referred to, especially in Europe or in racing circles, as simply "dampers."

For a practical example, just take any light coil spring a few inches long. Hold it up by one end and attach a small weight to the lower end. The effect of gravity on the weight and the resistance of the spring will find a balanced position and the weight will stay where it is as though it were on the end of a piece of string. Now pull the weight down a short distance and let it go.

What happens?

In this case the spring is extended, so the weight will be pulled briskly upward. At the top of its path it will be applying more force (due to gravity) than the spring, so it will drop again and this oscillating, up and down movement will go on for quite a time, getting smaller and smaller, until finally twitching to a halt at the balanced position.

Without a damper, the wheel of a car would do the same thing. Indeed, you will occasionally see a car on the road that, having run over a bump, has a wheel going up and down almost uncontrollably—a sure sign that the damper or shock absorber is broken or simply worn out.

Ideally, the job of the shock absorber is to allow the wheel to bounce into the air against the spring pressure when it runs over a bump and then stop it at the balanced position as the spring pushes it back down again.

You can do a simple test at home to see if your shock absorbers are in good condition. At each corner (i.e., at each wheel of the car) give a brisk downward shove on the fender. If the shock absorber is in good condition, that corner should simply go down and then immediately come straight back up and stop at its original position. It will need quite a bit of force, since the shock absorber

has resistance in both directions and will therefore add to the bump resistance of the spring. In fact, if you are trying it on your Porsche and the shock absorbers are in good condition, you will probably need the assistance of a friend to get any noticeable body movement!

Antisway Bars

The third part of the suspension is the antisway, or antiroll, bar. It is connected to each wheel hub assembly with a flexible joint and also to the chassis through two bearing-type clamps, as far to the outside as possible, which will allow it to rotate, but not move, relative to the chassis.

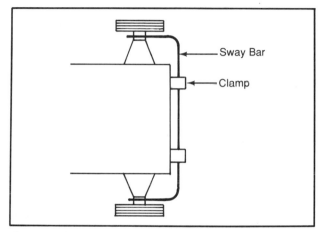

Antisway bar and clamp setup.

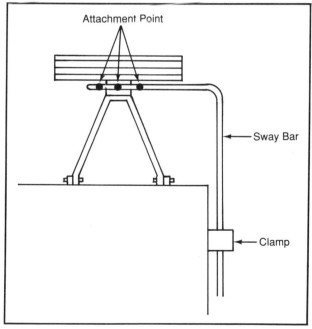

The variable attachment points that can effectively stiffen or soften the sway bar.

65

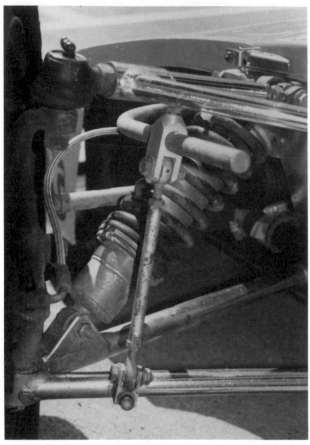

The combination of spring, shock absorber and sway bar assembly on a Formula Ford. Pete Lyons

Like the springs and shock absorbers, it is passive. It cannot do anything on its own but only react when something is done to it. When a car is cornering, the suspension will allow the mass of the vehicle to "roll" toward the outside. The outside springs will compress and the shock absorbers will dampen the movement so that the car takes on a set position. While the spring and shock absorber are being compressed, the end of the antisway bar at that particular wheel is being pushed up.

While the outside spring and shock absorber are being compressed, it follows that the lighter load allows the inside ones to extend. Hence the rolling motion of the car. Since the antisway bar is free to rotate in its bearings on the chassis of the car, it is clear that as the outside end is being pushed up, the inside end is also pushing up on the other wheel. In other words, it is limiting the amount that wheel will descend and therefore the amount the car will roll. How much it limits the rolling depends on its stiffness, or thickness, since it will twist.

As a simple experiment to get the idea of what is happening, unravel an ordinary paper clip. Get someone to hold the straight, center part down with two fingers, simulating the mounting points on the chassis. Then push up on one end while applying a downward pressure on the other end. The end you are pushing up on represents the outside wheel, which is trying to transmit that upward push to the other wheel. Of course, paper clips are

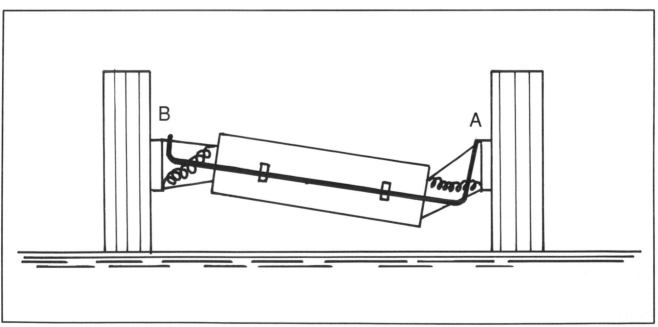

In a cornering situation, the outside sway bar attachment 'A' is forced upward by the rolling of the chassis. This will have the effect of pushing the inside sway bar *attachment 'B' upward, re-compressing the inside spring and restricting the amount of roll of the chassis.*

not very thick so there will be considerable torsional force and only a comparatively small fraction of the upward force can be transmitted to the other end before it starts to twist. But if your paper clip was half an inch thick, a much greater percentage of the force could be transmitted. On competition cars and indeed on some high-quality performance cars like Porsche, different thickness antisway bars are available that help the driver adjust the car to his or her liking according to the road conditions.

When a car starts to turn into a corner, there is a rolling and therefore shifting of weight toward the outside front tire. This loads the outside tire more than the inside one and allows it to do most of the steering.

If we were to stiffen up the suspension resistance of the front wheels, there would be less roll, less weight transfer to the outside wheel, and ultimately, less steering available. The car, instead of turning into the corner, would tend to go straight on, or at least have a much larger turning arc than that desired. That would be an example of the *understeering* condition mentioned in chapter 4.

If you did the opposite and softened the front suspension, the car would roll more, have more weight transfer to the outside wheel, which in turn would have more grip and the car would turn sharper than desired. That would be an *oversteering* condition.

So you can see that the adjustment from oversteer to understeer, or vice versa, can be controlled

Porsche 908/3, Nürburgring, 1970
My second Nürburgring 1000km victory, in a 908/3. Note the extreme driver-forward position, which gave su-

perb driver visibility, especially valuable on tracks like the Nürburgring and the Targa Florio. H. P. Seufert

by fairly simple chassis adjustments. Softening or stiffening the front springs is one way to make the adjustment. Easier still, just change the antisway bar, or simply make the antisway bar itself softer or stiffer. Most competition cars have an adjustment available, whereby simply moving the point of attachment, you increase or decrease the leverage.

What you are doing in this situation is increasing or decreasing the force being transmitted through the bar to the opposite wheel. The magnitude of this force is controlled by the torque or "twisting force" applied to the bar. Torque is measured in lb-ft (force in pounds multiplied by distance in feet) and since all other aspects of the rolling action of the car are constant, you can see that when the antisway bar is at its "softest," the force being transmitted to the other side will be smallest. When it is at its "stiffest," it follows that the force will be greatest.

Remember that Porsches, most other performance cars, and virtually all competition cars have antisway bars at both front and rear. Doing something to one of them does the opposite to the other one. If, therefore, you are trying to adjust the car to have more understeer, you could increase the stiffness of the front antisway bar. But you could also decrease the stiffness of the rear antisway bar. Or you could do a combination of the two!

Tuning Suspension

Shock absorber adjustment is more delicate and usually involves the up and down balance of front and rear or a combination of both. It is usually not available on production cars, but for those seeking performance beyond that provided by the manufacturer, many high-quality performance accessories are available. In the case of Porsche, many can be found in the manufacturer's catalog or, especially for 911 models, through aftermarket suppliers.

Nürburgring, 1970
My second 1000km victory was won with Kurt Ahrens.
Eric della Faille

Porsche 911, Stuttgart-Lyon-Charbonnières, 1967
Note the body roll due to weight transfer—it shows up dramatically here on the rally-prepared and therefore softer sprung 911. We were on the way to victory at Lyon-Charbonnières. Vic Elford collection

In the case of shock absorbers, for example, you will find models with one single adjustment that stiffens or softens both "bump" and "rebound" equally. "Bump" is the resistance when the wheel is bumped up. "Rebound" is the resistance to the wheel dropping back from the "bump" position.

You will also find even more sophisticated, and therefore, more expensive models where bump and rebound can be adjusted independently. Again, depending on the sophistication required, some can be adjusted in place in a matter of seconds, while others have to be removed from the car. The choice is yours!

Perhaps you have already "breathed" on the engine in your car to give it greater acceleration. Now you have a car that squats heavily onto the rear wheels when you accelerate hard. The shock absorbers may be in perfectly good condition but just not set firmly enough to handle this extra performance. Carefully adjusting the bump of the rear shocks will return the car to an even keel.

If the front of the car rears in the air on acceleration, you can adjust the rebound of the front shock absorbers to help solve the problem. Similarly, if you have fitted oversize or otherwise higher performance tires, perhaps for autocrossing, you

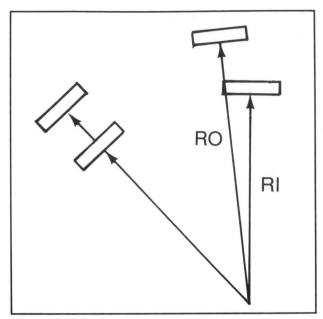

'RI' is the radius of the curve traveled by the inside wheel whereas 'RO' is the radius of the curve traveled by the outside wheel.

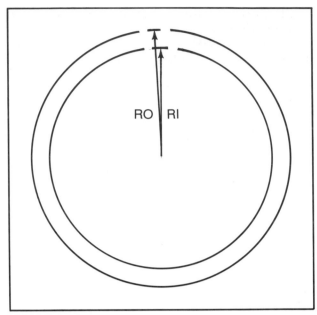

If the radius of the curve traveled by the inside wheel, 'RI,' is 100ft, the wheels will travel 632ft in a complete circle. If the car has a "track," i.e. the width between the wheels, of 5ft, the outside wheels will travel 659ft.

may find that the car will generate greater braking efficiency than before, causing the nose to dive and the rear to rise excessively under heavy braking. Now you have to do the opposite. Stiffen up the front bump and/or the rear rebound.

Remember that any time you adjust the shock absorbers, whether bump or rebound, whether on or off the car, *always* turn them back to the "zero" setting and adjust up again to the desired level. Unless you are driving under exceptional circumstances (and I cannot think of any that would apply, apart from driving on an oval), left and right front should have identical settings, as, of course, should left and right rear.

Of course, in the case of "diving" or "squatting," some of these adjustments can be achieved by changing spring rates. The limitation here is that springs only work one way, on compression. Any adjustment in the extension department can only be made on the shock absorber—or in extreme cases on the spring rates *at the other end* of the car!

Limited-Slip Differentials

Another thing that can greatly affect handling, particularly on surfaces with poor grip, is a limited-slip differential. When a car is negotiating a corner, it is obvious that the outside wheels must travel farther and therefore faster than the inside ones.

On the nondriven wheels, that is, the front ones on a rear-drive car, rear ones on a front-wheel- drive car, that is of little importance. The

wheels are not rigidly attached to each other so the outside one simply goes quicker than the inside one.

However, the driven wheels must be attached to each other. If they weren't, you would only be able to apply power to one wheel. The "attachment" is made by the "differential," which allows a difference in speed between one and the other.

But remember when I was discussing suspension and steering earlier, I explained that in order to negotiate a corner, there has to be a certain amount of body roll to make the steering work. That body roll is also present to a greater or lesser degree at the rear of the car. This means that as a car goes through a corner there is more weight on the outside wheels than the inside ones.

From the above description of the differential, you can see that any excess of power applied when the weight is on the outside wheel will allow the inside wheel to spin. While one wheel is spinning, *no power* is being transmitted to the other wheel. You have no alternative but to reduce power to the level that the more lightly loaded wheel can accept and you will not be able to use full power until the car has exited the corner onto the straight and resumed a perfectly balanced posture right to left.

Even then, if you are accelerating hard on a poor surface—a surface that has a mixture of wet and dry or a road that has sand or dust along the edge where the right wheels are, but is clean in the middle where the left ones are—there will be a constantly changing coefficient of friction between the two driven wheels, which will take turns spinning or gripping.

The limited-slip differential is designed to eliminate this constant slip/grip situation by locking the rear wheels together so that there is no differential, or at least only a predetermined, limited differential in speed between them. Even when one wheel suddenly has less grip than the other, it will still keep turning at the same, or close to the same, speed. One of them will still be spinning a little. On occasions both will be spinning, but they will both be transmitting almost equal power to the road and the driver will be able to use maximum acceleration while still keeping control of the car.

With a front-wheel-drive car, a limited-slip differential is usually a liability rather than a help. Once it has locked up, both wheels are turning at about the same speed, but the inside one has less distance to travel and tends to push the outside one beyond its ideal arc, creating a case of massive understeer. Recent technological advances have helped to correct that undesirable situation with a viscous coupling traction control, allowing a distribution of power between the front wheels rather than a complete lockup.

Once again, the almost unlimited budgets and technology of Formula 1 are taking us into the future in this respect. Many of the cars now use a sophisticated traction control device. A sensor at each driven wheel notifies a computer when it is about to lose traction, and the computer reduces the power being transmitted to that wheel only. Like the computerized suspension discussed earlier, these adjustments are made thousands of times a second, so whatever the conditions, the driver, just by putting a foot on the floor and letting the computer do the work, can always accelerate at the absolute limit of the car.

Traction control is also beginning to make an appearance on road-going cars, but for the most part is less sophisticated than that of Formula 1. In particular, whereas the racing version is what I would call "positive" control, most passenger car versions are what I would term "negative" control. In other words, while the racing version acts on the power, seeking to keep the maximum available at the wheels at all times, the road versions generally use the ABS sensors to apply the brake to the wheel that is trying to spin. (See chapter 8 for more information on ABS sensors.)

Chapter 6

The Tires

The place: A Welsh forest
The time: A cold, wet night in 1962
The occasion: Birmingham Post National Rally

I was flinging my little DKW with its screaming three-cylinder, 750cc two-stroke engine through the slippery, muddy logging tracks determined to win my second national rally in as many weeks. With the front wheels alternately sliding, spinning, and gripping on the slick surface we were once again outdistancing our competitors. The car was showing definite signs of contact with the scenery, but we did indeed make it back to Birmingham and our second successive victory.

My DKW was the only one running in the British rally championship, so although I could compare my performance against other drivers in other cars, I had no idea how I might fare against other DKWs. Until now, I had largely considered that the tires on a car were just there to keep the rims from scraping on the road and that the best ones were simply the cheapest ones!

A few weeks later I set off for my first real attempt at an international rally, the Tulip, where not for the last time, I was to learn that there is much more to driving than just sitting behind the wheel and pushing the pedals.

Because the DKW was such a fast and comparatively cheap car, a hoard of them entered the Tulip. I had put new tires on, of course, but they were the same large-diameter ones that I used in Britain, where good ground clearance is always important for the forest rallies. Here on the Tulip, all of the special stages were on paved hill climbs, which meant that we needed the lowest possible gearing. In fact, changing gears was not allowed in those days, and in any case, there were no alternatives available for the DKW, so the only thing to do was to put on the smallest possible diameter tires that effectively reduced the final-drive ratio.

The European DKW drivers who were used to competing against one another in such conditions already knew about little things like that and had all turned up with the tiniest tires available. All the way through the event I took a beating from the Europeans and went home a wiser man, determined never to overlook any possibility to make the car better in the future.

Today the choice of tires is almost embarrassingly large, from the purest of deep snow tires to treadless racing "slicks," and Goodyear is one of the most knowledgeable and advanced tire manufacturers as a result of its total continuous commitment to virtually every branch of motor sport for decades.

A tire can never do more than 100 percent of anything. It can be pushed to 100 percent of its capacity on braking or in cornering, or a combination of the two, but it can never go beyond 100 percent.

Tire Speed Ratings

If you are driving your Porsche in most European countries, even if their speed limit does not allow you to approach the maximum speed of the car, you must have it equipped with the appropriate "speed-rated" tires.

Speed ratings are given by the tire manufacturer to indicate the *maximum* sustained speed that can be used safely by that tire. The speed ratings that you need to know about for your Porsche or other sports car are probably those in the higher

Studded Hakaapelitaa winter tires from Finland. As you might imagine from their looks, they can only be used when the road is totally covered with ice and snow. I once used them on a Monte Carlo Rally special stage that was *a mixture of asphalt, ice, and snow, and although providing phenomenal performance, they were totally destroyed after 30 miles!* Gisbert Watermann

ranges. They are all marked somewhere on the tire, usually in the tire size description, and are shown by a letter:

Speed symbol	Maximum speed
H	130mph
V	149mph
Z	over 149mph

Tire Aspect Ratios

Also in the tire size description is an indication of the "aspect ratio." This shows how high the tire is in relation to its width. So a Goodyear Eagle ZR Gatorback radial on the rear of your 1992 Porsche 911 or 968 will probably be marked 225/50ZR16. The 50 shows that it has a 50 percent aspect ratio; in other words, it is twice as wide as it is high. The Z means that it is rated for sustained speeds above 149mph: the German autobahn, for example. Basically, the lower the aspect ratio of a tire, the better the cornering power it can generate.

Years ago, snow tires were very narrow in order to exert the maximum possible pressure and really "dig" through the snow as far as possible. Today's snow tires are usually not so narrow, but the deep grooves between the treads allow them to exert the same pressure, measured in pounds per square inch.

The Goodyear Eagle M + S, today's all-around high-performance winter tire. Goodyear

Tire Slip Angles

Whenever you read a driving handbook, you will read about tire slip angles, a concept that is both simple and extremely complicated at the same time. Simple to explain; complicated to analyze.

When the car is going along in a straight line, neither the wheel nor tire is affected by any side forces. When you start to turn into a corner, the wheel rim turns first. At that instant, the wheel is turned, but the tread of the tire is still pointing straight ahead on the road. The angle between the wheel rim and the tire tread is called the "slip angle." As the car continues into the corner, the slip angle may increase, stay the same, or decrease.

The greater the slip angle of the front wheels, the greater the understeer will be. In the diagram the wheel is turned hard to the right, but the tire less so. The greater the difference between the two (i.e., the slip angle) the greater the tendency for the tires to slide—or in this case, because the diagram shows the front tires—to understeer. This is further aggravated on a front-wheel-drive car because more weight is over the front wheels, which makes it more difficult for the tread patch on the road to follow the direction of the rim when the wheel is turned.

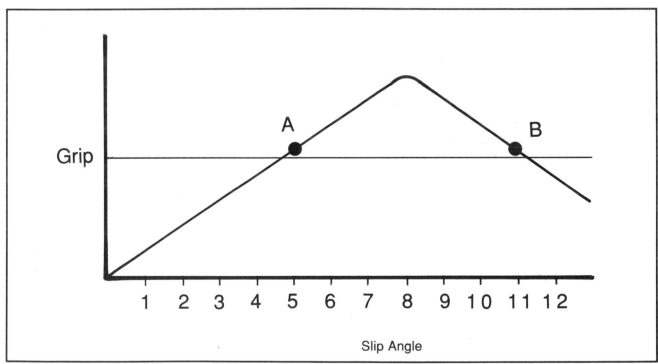

As the slip angle increases, so does the grip—up to a maximum of about 7–8 degrees. Beyond that point, the grip will decrease. It is obvious from the diagram that the driver using about a 5-degree slip angle 'A,' although he or she has not yet obtained the maximum grip, is much better placed to control the car than the driver at slip angle 'B.' Even though the grip in both cases is the same, at 'A' it still has room to increase whereas at 'B' it is already diminishing.

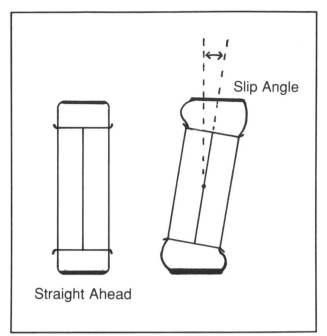

In the moment of transition from traveling straight ahead to cornering, the wheel has turned but the tire is still pointing straight ahead, creating the initial slip angle.

The Goodyear GS D is a Z rated directional tire, originally developed for the Porsche Carrera 2 and Carrera 4. Goodyear

The Goodyear Aquatred, specially developed for those who drive almost continually in wet conditions. It is directional, meaning it must rotate in one direction only, and is limited to S rated, family car, applications. Goodyear

The ultimate in dry road conditions—the Goodyear Eagle Formula 1 tire. Because the grip comes from the amount of rubber in contact with the road, there is no tread. The little holes are to enable the tire engineers to determine how much of the rubber has been used—or how much is left! Goodyear

The ultimate in the wet. The Goodyear Eagle Formula 1 rain tire, asymmetrical and directional. Goodyear

With a rear-wheel-drive car, the opposite can be true. A Porsche 911, as I have explained, has only about 40 percent of its weight on the front wheels, so they will turn and the tire will follow fairly easily, generating only a comparatively small slip angle. Because of this, the rear wheels will turn quickly, generating a large slip angle between them and the tires and causing the rear wheels to slide outward resulting in oversteering.

But whatever car you drive and whatever tires it has on it, a tire can never do more than 100 percent of anything. It can be pushed to 100 percent of its capacity on breaking or in cornering, or a combination of the two, but it can never go beyond 100 percent.

Remember this concept; it will come into focus when I discuss various aspects of handling in a later chapter.

Tire Pressures

Tire pressures are also vitally important to both performance and safety. Check them regularly and never let them descend below the manufacturer's recommended pressure. If you tend to drive in a spirited fashion and if you are going to be driving at sustained high speed, as you may legally do on the German autobahn, for example, it is probably a good idea to inflate the tires 2–4psi (pounds per square inch), but no more, over the recommended pressure. This will help to keep them cool.

Underinflation can be dangerous as it will cause the tires to overheat. Excessive overinflation, particularly with low-profile tires, will also cause overheating around the center of the tire tread. Either can cause a violent blowout, which at 150mph is likely to have disastrous consequences!

Chapter 7

Accelerating and Gear Changing

The place: Hockenheim racetrack
The time: 1973
The occasion: Solitude Interseries race

At the end of 1971, the Fédération International de l'Automobile had closed the loophole in the international sports car regulations

Porsche 917, 1969
All twenty-five "production" 917 sports cars lined up to be counted for homologation by the FIA. These were known as the "secretary" cars because they had been hastily assembled by anyone at the factory who could *hold a wrench! Needless to say, they were dismantled and rebuilt by the racing mechanics before ever setting foot, or in this case, wheel, on a racetrack! Werkfoto Porsche*

that had allowed such beautiful racing monsters as the Porsche 917 and the Ferrari 512 to be created. In fact, as far back as 1968, the FIA had started to show concern over the power and speed of prototype sports racing cars.

From 1969, racing prototypes would be limited to 3.0-liter engine capacity, effectively eliminating Ford GT 40s, Lolas with American V-8 power, and other such exotic cars.

A new class, to be known as the "Sports" category would be introduced, with a 5.0-liter engine capacity limit and a minimum production of twenty-five cars per year. The intention was to allow "real" production sports cars, made in small numbers, to compete internationally. By "real" sports cars, the FIA meant things that actually existed: Aston Martin, Chevrolet Corvette, and others.

Unfortunately for the FIA, it had not counted on the imagination of such men as Ferdinand Piëch of Porsche and Mauro Forghieri of Ferrari. Porsche was first, but ultimately both companies decided that they would build twenty-five 5.0-liter production sports (racing) cars.

Porsche duly presented the 917 at the Geneva Auto Show in 1969, where I fell in love with it at first sight. It was big, beautiful, and immensely powerful. By April, all twenty-five "production cars" were lined up in the courtyard at Stuttgart,

Porsche 917, Sebring, 1971
Just two years later the 917 had evolved into this beautifully balanced car. Here I am on the way to winning the 12 Hours of Sebring in 1971. Leonard Turner

Porsche 917, Daytona, 1971
Here I am in my 917 leading a Ferrari 512 into the in-field at the 1971 24 Hours of Daytona. Werkfoto Porsche

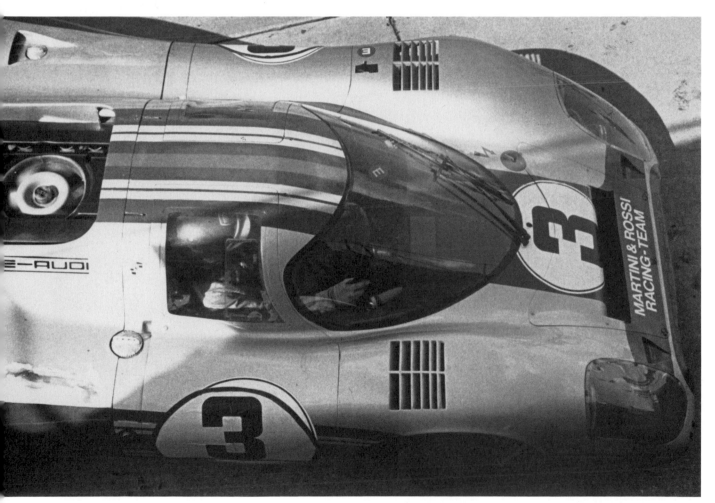

Porsche 917, Sebring, 1971
With aerodynamics beginning to play a major role in sports car design, the drivers compartment was a tight *fit! As you have seen from other photos, I am 5ft 10in and of slight build, but even for me the 917 was a bit of a squeeze.* Leonard Turner

to be counted by FIA officials in time for homologation for the Le Mans race of that year. Whether they all worked or not has always been open to discussion, but there they were.

Even at that speed there was so much power that the 917/30 left two black lines on the road from the spinning rear wheels for about 50 yards as it accelerated toward the next corner.

Rumor has it that at Ferrari, where the parts were built in a number of different departments spread around Maranello and Modena, they got all the pieces together to assemble the cars and found that they actually had enough to make twenty-six instead of just the twenty-five needed!

Now I was at Hockenheim at the wheel of perhaps the greatest racing car ever built. During its three-year reign, the 917, in all its forms, had dominated the world championship sports car racing scene as no other car had ever done before.

After the removal of the 917 from the world championship, Porsche had started setting its sights on the American Can-Am series. With the turbocharged 917/10, it had already had its first successes in the Can-Am in the hands of Hurley Haywood.

The car I was now sitting in was known as the 917/10-30. It was, in fact, a rolling test bed of the car that had recently gone to the United States for Mark Donohue and George Follmer, who were already starting to sweep everything before them in the Can-Am.

Today it was running in 917/30 configuration, with long wheelbase and a 5.4-liter turbocharged engine developing over 1200hp!

Waiting, 1969
Being a racing driver isn't all action.... Jutta Fausel

The reason I was there was that the Inter-series in Europe, like the Can-Am for so many years before it, was being dominated by just two cars and two drivers, Willi Kauhsen and Leo Kinnunen, both in 917 turbos. The organizers decided they would like to add a little spice to the event and persuaded Porsche that now that the test bed 917/10-30 had fulfilled its experimental role, it should go racing. The fact that the chairman of the race organizing committee was Ed Peter, manager of Porsche's export sales department, may have

Winning, 1971
...And sometimes you need something other than a steering wheel in your hand! Vic Elford collection

Yawning, 1971
...Sometimes it's just plain boring.... Eberhard Strähle

had something to do with the fact that Porsche agreed!

Neither I nor anyone else had ever driven a car like the 917/30. For perhaps the first time ever in the history of automobile racing, the engineers had what amounted to almost unlimited horse-power, which meant that they could add a phenomenal amount of downforce to the car. You can get an idea of how much from the photographs, which show the big shovel nose and a rear wing nearly the size of a dining room table. The effect of the aerodynamics here at Hockenheim were such that at 180mph the car developed over one ton of downforce!

I had set the fastest time in practice and had Willi beside me on the front row of the grid and Leo tucked in behind as we came up to take the flag at the rolling start.

In those early days of turbocharging the "turbo lag," or the response time between opening the

Porsche 917/30, Hockenheim, 1973
Almost unlimited downforce! Eberhard Strähle

throttle and the engine developing power, was quite considerable. I am sure that the engineers had measured it and could put an exact figure to it. As a driver, I measured it more by instinct and reaction, and I would guess it to be about two-tenths of a second. Just the blink of an eye, you might think, and not worth worrying about. Except that in a race car you must judge the exact turn-in and acceleration points for a corner within inches, and at 120mph you travel 35ft in two-tenths of a second!

Whenever you apply the power for acceleration, you must do so in a smooth transition. Any change in the car's dynamic condition must be done following a parabolic curve.

I had talked to Norbert Singer, the factory engineer in charge of the car, about getting a jump at the start. If I waited for the green flag and then buried the accelerator, I would have to wait about two-tenths of a second before anything happened. "Could I approach the start with my left foot on the brake to hold the speed down and my right foot on the gas pedal to keep the turbo pressure up?" I asked. "Well, you can try," was the response, "but Willi and Leo have tried, and they can't hold onto the car."

I tried it a couple of times during practice and it felt all right, so I decided to do it for the start of the race. Carefully balancing my two feet on brake and accelerator pedals, all I had to do as the green flag waved was take my foot off the brake and put the accelerator to the floor. The turbo pressure was already there and with something like an instant 1000hp, the car took off like a rocket. Norbert had been right. Wheel spin in first, then second, then third gears and tiny but rapid corrections to the steering to keep the car pointing more or less in a straight line kept me busy all the way to the first corner. But not having had to wait for the power to build up meant that when I got there, I was already leading by 50 yards!

Performance driving means being able to drive fast and safely, but it also means driving in such a way that the car is not being ill-treated mechanically.

Out through the first right-left-right chicane where I had to judge the moment to put my foot back on the gas pedal some 10 yards before I needed the power, then on to the Ost Kurve. There was no chicane there in those days, and I would change up into fourth (top) gear at the exit of the corner at about 150mph. Even at that speed there was so much power that the car left two black lines on the road from the spinning rear wheels for about 50 yards as it accelerated toward the next corner.

Smooth Acceleration

Acceleration like that of the 917/30 is exhilarating beyond words, but it must be treated with respect and carefully controlled. Whenever you apply the power for acceleration, you must do so in a smooth transition. Never try to go from no power to maximum power instantaneously by just flooring the gas pedal. To do so will mean that you unbalance the car and risk losing control. Any change in the car's dynamic condition must be done following a parabolic curve.

For those of you who are not engineers, that probably sounds horribly complicated.

It's not.

Porsche 917/30, Hockenheim, 1973
Although shortened by the telephoto lens, the first corner lead was substantial. Vic Elford collection

Porsche 917/30, Hockenheim, 1973
You can almost feel the power emanating from the
917/30. Eberhard Strähle

As with everything else, applying the power must be done *smoothly*. If the car you drive has a great deal of power, trying to get it all to the road in one go will probably result in wheel spin or even spinning the car. You must start gently and increase the power according to a parabolic curve as the speed increases. The faster you are going, the more rapidly you can increase the power.

Of course, apart from starting, the application of power usually comes after negotiating a corner. The technique of cornering is discussed in detail in chapter 10, but for the moment, I will discuss acceleration out of a corner.

Remember in chapter 6 I talked about a tire being able to do only 100 percent of something? That leaves us in the theoretical position of being able to use absolute maximum power only when the car is going in a straight line. While it is in a corner, you can apply some power to exit the corner, but the amount is limited by the amount of steering you are using.

A simple way to understand this is to imagine a piece of string with one end tied around the big toe of your right foot, which is absolutely flat on the gas pedal. The string is drawn tight and the other end is attached to the bottom of the steering

84

Mark Donohue, Porsche 917/30, Road Atlanta, 1973
Mark Donohue leads the 1973 Can-Am field down through the Road Atlanta esses in the superb Penske-Sunoco Porsche 917/30. Werkfoto Porsche

wheel. As long as you are going in a straight line, all is well, but as soon as the steering wheel is turned, you can no longer stay flat on the gas. If you use a quarter of a turn of the steering wheel to take the corner, the string will pull your right foot way back from the floor. It is only as the car begins to straighten out after the corner that the string will allow the right foot to go progressively back to maximum throttle.

Synchronizing Gear Changes

Performance driving means being able to drive fast and safely, but it also means driving in such a way that the car is not being ill-treated mechanically. It is amazing how many novice drivers think that getting the most out of a car on acceleration means snatching the gear lever from one gear to the next with as much force and speed as they can muster.

All modern cars have a system inside the gearbox called synchromesh. It does exactly what its

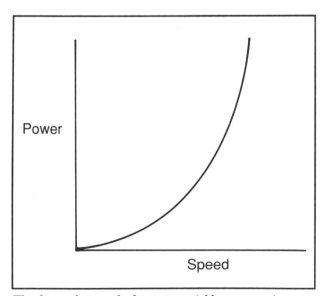

The faster the speed, the more quickly you can increase power.

name implies and *synchronizes* the *meshing* of the gears. In fact, many, many cars use a Porsche synchromesh system, which was pioneered by Dr. Porsche in the 1930s and patented and sold under license to the majority of the world's automakers for decades.

For example, if the engine input shaft is turning at 5000rpm and the transmission output shaft is turning at 3000rpm, moving to the next higher gear will require the output shaft to remain at 3000rpm but the input shaft speed will drop to (say) 4000rpm. The synchromesh cones move ahead of the input gear so that when the latter arrives, it is turning at the correct speed to mesh with the constantly turning output gear. Trying to change gear faster than the synchromesh can do its job will mean a noisy clashing of teeth, excessive wear and tear on both the synchromesh and the gears, and eventually a premature, expensive transmission rebuild!

Most racing cars do not have synchromesh, for a variety of reasons. First it adds weight and race car designers are constantly striving to get down to a weight limit. If they are able to design their cars to be under the weight limit for a particular formula, they then have the luxury of being able to add the necessary weight to make the car legal, exactly where they want it in order to give the best possible balance and performance.

The second reason synchromesh is rarely used on race cars, is that a skilled driver can actually synchronize the gear speeds faster than the synchromesh can do it. Every engine has a flywheel attached to the crankshaft that helps to keep the engine turning smoothly. The one on your road car is comparatively heavy, so that when you put your foot on the throttle it will take a little time for the engine to "wind up" through the rev range. Conversely, when you lift your foot from the throttle at high speed, the momentum of the flywheel will

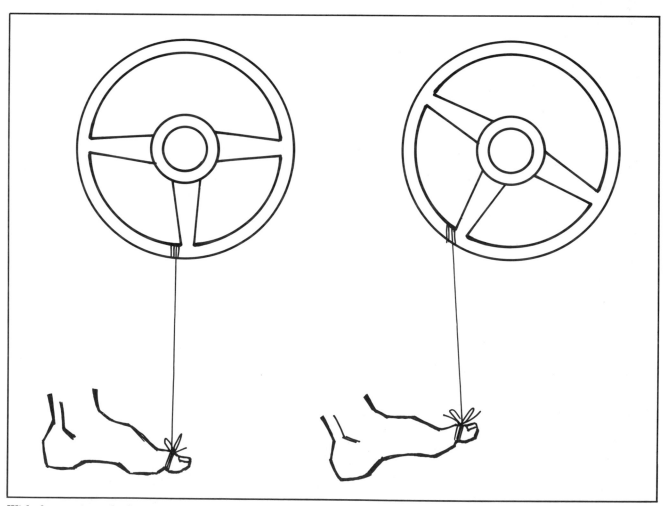

With the steering wheel straight ahead, left, the foot can be flat on the floor. With steering wheel turned in a corner, right, the string will stop the foot going all the way to the floor.

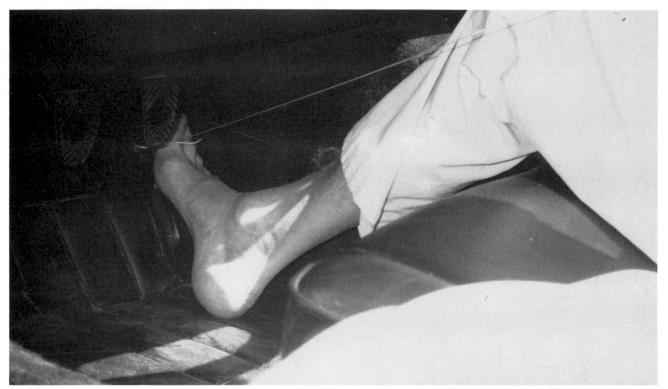

Tie a string from the steering wheel to your big toe as a test. With the steering wheel straight ahead, the string allows full throttle. Whether it is on the throttle or the brake pedal, the position of the foot is governed by the amount of steering being used.

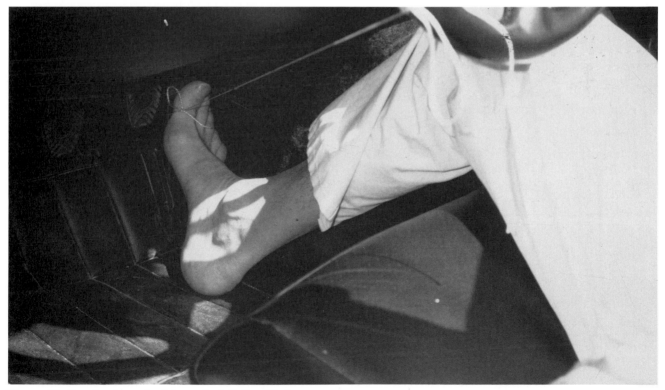

Now with the steering wheel turned, full throttle is no longer possible.

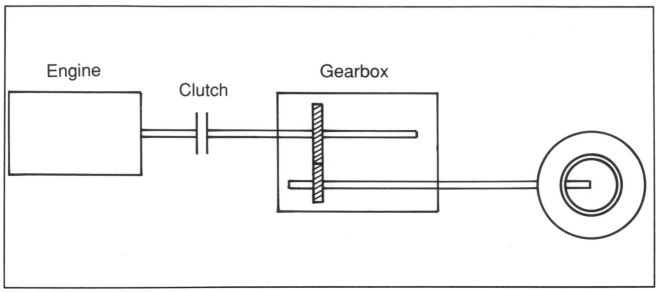

Typical engine-clutch-gearbox layout.

only allow the engine to slow down comparatively slowly.

The flywheel on a pure racing engine, on the other hand, is relatively light, which means that opening the throttle allows the engine to speed up very quickly and closing it gives very rapid engine deceleration. These rapid changes in engine speed also help to account for the fact that the racing dri-

During a gear change, the entire cluster of gears on the input shaft moves. The synchromesh cones on the output shaft are connected to the input gears and move ahead of them, mating into the output gears so that the output gears are speeded up or slowed down to exactly match the speed of the input gear when it arrives.

ver, or to be more precise, the good driver driving a pure racing car, can often change gear quicker without synchromesh.

So when you are accelerating hard in your Porsche and you change from first to second gear at maximum revs, don't thrust or grab the gear lever as hard and as fast as you can. Move it firmly but gently and you will actually be able to feel the synchronizers at work as they match the gear speeds within the transmission and allow the next pair of gears to mesh smoothly together.

If you are driving a race car (or a truck) without synchromesh, you really need to learn how to double declutch in order to perform smooth, noiseless changes, a technique discussed in the next chapter.

Despite the advantages of "straight cut" or nonsynchromesh gears for racing, Porsche, as the inventor of synchromesh, always used synchromesh gearboxes in all its racing cars. In the case of the 917, especially the turbo versions, the gearboxes were of massive construction in order to cope with the power. I, along with many of the other factory drivers, pleaded constantly with the engineers to give us nonsynchro transmissions so that we could change gears faster and lower our lap times. But such was the integrity of people like Piëch that they steadfastly refused. Their argument was that racing both developed and showcased the breed. Anything that was developed from racing and could ultimately find its way into a production car, would. Similarly, any past development now used in road cars but that could also be incorporated into the racing program, where it would undergo even further development, would do so as well.

Smooth Gearshifts

For this example, let us just use a synchromesh gearbox for the moment. Accelerating as fast as possible, the revs in first gear will quickly reach maximum. As they do, the change to second gear must be done with careful coordination of both feet as well as the gear lever. The right foot should release the gas pedal at the same instant as the left foot declutches. By declutching, I mean pushing the clutch pedal in to the stop. While these two actions are taking place, the gear lever can be moved into the neutral position.

Then continuing the movement of the gear lever towards the next gear, a slight resistance will be felt as the synchromesh cones go to work. As soon as this resistance diminishes, the gear lever will slip smoothly into the next gear. At this point the clutch pedal should be let out and the throttle pedal put smoothly down so that there is a perfect match of gear speed and engine speed as the clutch is fully home. If the car lurches nose down as your foot comes off the clutch, you did not have enough gas. If the engine and clutch spin, you had too much gas.

Try it at low speeds first until you are absolutely sure you can get it right every time. Then slowly work up to maximum revs.

Now let's do it without synchromesh. You will see from the diagrams that although the gears still slide back and forth on their respective shafts, there are no synchromesh cones attached to them. You must use the engine to adjust the speed of the revolving gears so that they will mesh smoothly together. Incidentally, even though your road-going Porsche has synchromesh, you can still go through the motions of changing gear without synchro.

Now the sequence is as follows:

1. Right foot off the gas pedal, left foot in on the clutch pedal, gear lever to neutral (all three actions taking place simultaneously).

2. Left foot out from the clutch pedal, which will adjust the gearbox input shaft to the new, slower, engine speed.

3. Left foot in on the clutch and gear lever immediately into the next gear position.

4. Clutch pedal out and throttle pedal down as before.

Chapter 8

Braking and Heel-and-Toe Gear Changing

The place: Sebring
The time: 1971
The occasion: Sebring 12 hours race

My second ever visit to the United States was for the Sebring race in 1968 and a second place with Jochen Neerpasch. The race in 1969 was less kind; a broken chassis led to a bizarre-handling car that Richard Attwood and I could only bring home in seventh place.

The 1970 race was even worse. Sam Posey in a Ferrari 512 and I in the Porsche Austria 917 were both taken out by the inattentive driving of someone in one of the numerous small Italian cars. I was behind Sam, preparing to lap him, when we came up behind a 911 on the approach to the hairpin. We followed the 911 around the corner, and as it accelerated along the left side of the road, Sam and I went to the right (inside). Ahead of us on the inside was a little Italian car, and just as Sam had cleared the 911 and I was alongside it, preparing to flick left and right to go past the Italian, the latter suddenly braked.

Both Sam and I were much too close and going much too fast to be able to stop. Sam swerved to the right and went off the road, and although he was able to get back to the pits, the damage to his car was such that his race was over.

I swerved left and tried to make it through the rapidly diminishing gap between the Italian and the still accelerating 911, but there just wasn't room. There was a rending crash as my left rear wheel hit the right front fender of the 911 and I spun. I got going again, thinking that I had probably just punctured a tire, and made my way slowly back to the pits. This was in the days before crew/driver radios, so the mechanics were surprised to see me limp slowly into the pit lane.

As I rolled to a stop in front of the pit, the mechanics rushed around to the rear of the car—and then did nothing. Peter Falk, the engineer in charge of my car came back and opened my door. Leaning in he said, "You've lost a wheel." Frustrated at the delay, I remember saying, "So, put another one on!" "No, you don't understand, the entire rear corner has gone; wheel, suspension, brake, driveshaft…. There is nothing there to attach a wheel to!"

As I had tried to pull out in front of the 911, its front bumper had gone inside the middle of my wheel and simply ripped it completely off, taking everything else with it.

Sam and I roamed the pit lane after the incident, hoping to lay eyes and, frankly, hands on the culprit. But the incident had happened so quickly that neither of us had seen the car's number. All we could remember was that it was a little red Italian car. We didn't even know if it was an Alfa Romeo, a Fiat, or a Lancia! Perhaps fortunately for the driver, we never found him.

Now a year later, I was back in my favorite state, Florida. You'll remember that I cannot stand the cold, and for me anything under 75 degrees Fahrenheit is cold! That's one of the reasons I like Florida so much. That and the easygoing lifestyle where there is always plenty of time and no one is ever in a hurry.

Once a year the sleepy little town of Sebring comes alive and the restaurants resounds with as much French, German, and Italian as English. All the foreigners get to try grits for breakfast, usually only once, and with the medical check performed on the second floor of the local fire station, we got to slide down the fire fighter's emergency pole through the hole in the floor when it was over!

To crown it all, the technical inspection was also carried out downtown, so those who chose to do so also got to drive their race cars the six miles or so to the circuit, escorted by the local police and sheriffs departments!

Porsche had been spending too much money on racing over the last few years, and starting in

Porsche 908, Sebring, 1969
The last Le Mans-type start at Sebring in 1969. Obviously the open cockpit of the Porsche 908s gave their drivers an advantage. Here Jo Siffert is already in front, followed by Gerhardt Mitter in number 29 and myself in number 30. Bill Warner/Dennis Kirkland

Porsche 917, Sebring, 1971
The start of the 1971 Sebring 12 Hours.... Leonard Turner

1970 the "official" factory team was run by John Wyer. With lead drivers Jo Siffert and Pedro Rodriguez, it was a formidable combination.

In 1970, I had signed for the Porsche Austria Team but after one year that too had disappeared. Martini & Rossi came to the rescue for the 1971 season. Having been present as a sponsor for many years, they had gone one step further and created the Martini Racing Team with factory support from Porsche, and I was now driving for them.

Daytona in 1971 had been an expensive disaster for the Martini team, with both cars suffering severe damage, and we were reduced to just one car for Sebring. After having passed many years as friends and fierce competitors, I now found myself with Gerard Larrousse as my codriver.

The race started with what had become almost a tradition: a fierce no-holds-barred fight between Siffert, Rodriguez, and me, only this time we had Mark Donohue in Roger Penske's Ferrari 512 and Mario Andretti in the new factory Ferrari 312 joining the party. The 512 was already a strong contender in the world championship, and the 312 had made a sensational debut in Argentina just a few weeks earlier. The question was no longer which Porsche would win, but whether it would be a Porsche or a Ferrari.

Early in the race, while running wheel to wheel with Pedro, I had my first scare. With Pedro in front, the nose of my car tucked in literally inches from his gearbox, we caught a slower car as we came into the heavy braking area at the end of one of the long airfield runway straights. The driver, seeing a 917 looming in his mirrors, politely let Pedro past on the entry to the corner. Unfortunately, he had seen only one 917, not two, and as soon as Pedro had gone by, he took his line into the apex of the corner, chopping off part of my left front fender and sending us both into a spin!

Memories of my three-wheeled 917 from the year before flooded my mind, but this time, after nothing more than a quick unscheduled pit stop to tape up the nose, we were running again and slowly reeling in the leaders. The task was made easier when Jo's 917 ran out of gas on the circuit, Pedro and Mark were racing so fiercely that they collided, necessitating long pit stops for both, and Mario had an oil cooler break.

Porsche 917, Sebring, 1971
...And here I am having a busy time threading my way through traffic. Leonard Turner

Porsche 917, Sebring, 1971
Here we are being interviewed by Chris Economaki after Gerard Larrousse finally made it to victory lane! Vic Elford collection

This left two Alfa Romeos in first and second place. But they were no match for the Martini Racing 917, and before half distance, Gerard and I were firmly in the lead, never to lose it.

Lap after lap, day and night, the chassis and, above all, the brakes, were tested to their limits as we had to repeatedly slow the car from speeds approaching 200mph on the unbelievably rough concrete surface. But apart from one small delay in changing a recalcitrant brake pad, everything ran like clockwork and the Martini 917 was still stopping as well after twelve hours as it had at the start of the race.

Since I had started the race, the honor of receiving the checkered flag fell to Gerard. The entire Martini team watched and cheered as he crossed the finish line and set off on his victory lap. I headed for victory lane and the podium to wait for him...and wait...After what seemed an eternity, he finally arrived, and as we were re-ceiving the victory garlands and champagne, he confided sheepishly in my ear that he had been so excited at winning his first world championship race that he had spun on the cooling down lap!

Smooth Braking

In the last chapter we saw how important smoothness is in accelerating. If anything, smoothness is even more important when it comes to braking at the limit, also known as "threshold braking," since it means holding the braking absolutely at the threshold of the limit while still keeping control and not locking wheels.

Imagine for the moment that you are driving along a rain-swept, slippery highway at 65mph, a wet racetrack, or a German autobahn at 150mph. Imagine also that you are driving a Porsche 911, an older one without ABS, which in static form has only about 40 percent of its weight on the front wheels.

Because of an obstruction on the road or an approaching corner on the racetrack, you need maximum braking. If you slam your foot as hard as possible on the brake pedal, what will happen?

If you replied, "The wheels, at least the front ones, will lock up and the car will just slide," you are right. If you answered, "The car will spin," you are not necessarily right.

If the road is flat and you are going absolutely straight, then the car will not spin. Some outside influence must act on the car for it to spin. If the road is steeply cambered, for example, or if you are in a corner, then it probably will spin.

Smoothness is essential when it comes to braking at the limit since it means holding the braking absolutely at the threshold of the limit while still keeping control and not locking wheels.

Some of you have probably been told by well-meaning but misinformed friends that the best way to stop from high speed or under difficult conditions is by so-called "cadence" braking: stabbing away at the brake pedal, possibly even locking up at least the front wheels from time to time, with the car lurching forward and backward under the constant weight transfer.

But even locking up the front wheels and sliding is dramatic enough. Not only will you not slow down very quickly, I have even heard people say that the car speeds up when that happens, although that, of course, is not true. What is true is that the rate of deceleration decreases tremendously so it *feels* as though the car is speeding up,

but with the front wheels locked, you can no longer steer the car. Whatever you do with the steering wheel will have no effect whatsoever, the car will still go straight on.

In order to avoid locking up the front wheels, you must first add weight to them before braking heavily. In the chapter on balance I talked about the weight transfer from rear to front that occurs when you use the brakes. The chart shows a brake pressure scale of zero to ten. Zero is when the car is just rolling along neutrally. No acceleration, no deceleration. Ten is when the brakes are on and the wheels are absolutely at the limit of adhesion. The tiniest increase in pedal pressure and they will lock.

Although I have emphasized the importance of smoothness, here is one time when you need a little abrupt stab or jab. When your foot goes to the brake pedal, the first movement should be just that: a little jab at about four on the scale above.

That little jab will take up the pressure in the braking system and cause an instant weight transfer toward the front wheels. As soon as that is done, you can start squeezing on the brake pedal in earnest. The pressure with which you squeeze should increase according to a parabolic curve, just

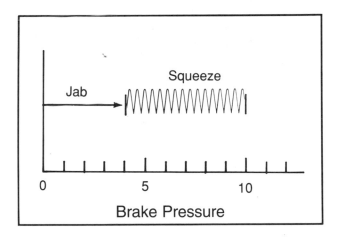

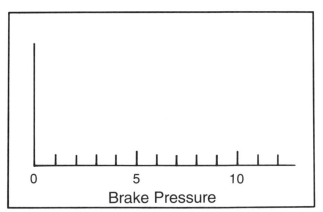

A simple graph for measuring brake pressure.

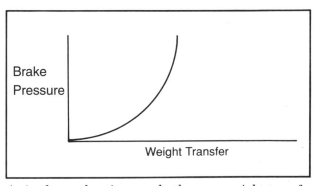

As in the acceleration graph, the more weight transfer there is toward the front of the car, the more rapidly you can increase brake pressure.

as when you are accelerating. The harder you squeeze, the more weight you put on the front wheels. The more weight on the front wheels, the harder you can squeeze, all the way up to ten on the scale.

When you try this the first time, one of three things will happen. Actually, there are four things that could happen, the fourth being that you get it right first time!

1. The jab will be fine, somewhere around four on the scale, but you squeeze...and squeeze...and squeeze...right off the end of the scale to about the

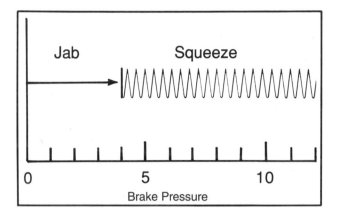

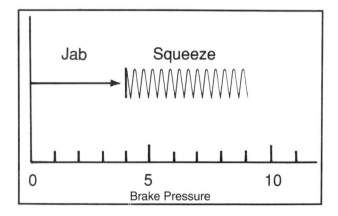

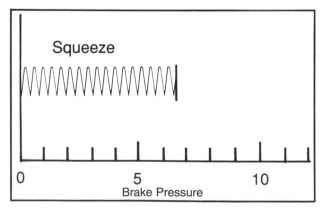

twelve position or beyond. By then, of course, the wheels have been locked up for a long time. If that happens, you must not come off the brake completely or you will have a reverse weight transfer toward the back of the car, the front wheels will be unloaded, and you literally have to start all over again. What you must do is "unsqueeze" the pedal, which will keep the weight over the front wheels and eventually release the brake pressure just enough so that the wheels are turning again.

In fact, if you are one of those people who push way beyond the ten on the scale and lock the wheels up, there is almost always a physical reason for that happening. In chapter 1 I emphasized the importance of comfort. To be comfortable when braking, you should be able to simply rotate your right foot from the throttle pedal to the brake pedal. The heel of the foot should stay on the floor, perhaps sliding a little to the left if necessary. If you use your entire leg to lift your foot up off the throttle, move it to the left, and then put it down again, you will almost certainly push too hard and lock the wheels. Why? Because using a leg action brings into play the very powerful but very insensitive muscles in the thigh. If those muscles are providing the pushing power, they are unable to make the fine pressure adjustments necessary. If you find that you do indeed have a tendency to use your leg so that all the thigh muscle power is pushing on the pedal in a straight line, then change the way you sit a little.

Lean your right leg out to the right so that the knee is well bent and practice rotating your foot as opposed to moving your leg. You can even hold your knee in place with your right hand a few times so that it is physically impossible to move it and, as you did before with the anticipation exercise, talk to yourself out loud.

Another advantage of splaying your knee out like that is that the thigh muscle cannot push around corners, so it is effectively taken out of operation.

In a tight-fitting racing car it is, of course, not possible to splay your leg out to the right, but you should still rotate your foot from one pedal to the other, don't lift it up and put it down again. With a Formula 1 car, you will need some force from the thigh muscles because the size and grip of the tires, allied to the incredible down force, necessitates very high pressure to get to the limits of the brakes. But by the time you get into a Formula 1 car you will already have had a lot of experience in developing your overall sensitivity!

2. You get the jab about right, then start squeezing on the pedal until you reach somewhere around the seven or eight level and then stop there.

Why? Purely psychological. If you have never been close to the braking limits of your Porsche before, your mind is simply not prepared for how well it will, in fact, stop. So you just need to practice a few times until you become accustomed to the braking performance available. As you increase the pressure and approach the 10 level, the tires will start to "chirp" a little, and you will feel them *almost* locking as the wheels seem to be going around in little jerky motions when you are absolutely at the limit of braking.

3. The third possibility is what I like to call "limousine driver" braking. No stab, no jab, just very, very gentle, smooth squeezing on the pedal. When you get to around six or seven on our scale, the wheels are going to lock up anyway, no matter how smooth and gentle you are!

Why? Because without the little jab, there was no weight transfer to the front wheels. They are still relatively unloaded, and it is therefore impossible to apply much brake pressure.

(There is, in fact, one very special circumstance where "cadence" braking *is* the most effective way to stop, which I will discuss later.)

Double Declutch Downshifting

In the last chapter I discussed the importance of matching engine and transmission speeds when changing gears during acceleration. This is even more important when changing to a lower gear, especially when changing gears *and* braking simultaneously.

But, one step at a time.

Let us start with double declutch downshifting.

Imagine you are driving along in your Porsche at 4000rpm in fifth gear and decide that you need

the extra acceleration that fourth gear provides. Since at the moment of changing to the lower gear the road speed will not change, you must adjust the engine speed. Suppose that 4000rpm in fifth gear is the equivalent of 5000rpm in fourth gear. To change gear, you must push the clutch in at the same time as you lift off the gas pedal; almost simultaneously you move the gear lever from fifth to the neutral position and then smoothly into fourth gear, remembering to let the synchromesh cones do their work.

By now, the engine speed will have dropped to idle, and if you let the clutch out, the wheels and transmission will have to speed the engine up to 5000rpm. You can do it that way, but letting the clutch out quickly will result in a screech of protest from the driven wheels, and car will try to stand on its nose. Letting the clutch out slowly will help, but it is still uncomfortable and will unbalance the car. In either case, if the road is slippery, you have a very good chance of locking the rear wheels momentarily, which could well send you into a spin or, in front wheel drive car, send you straight on, out of control.

The best, and correct, way to do it, having accomplished the actual gear change, is to give a little "blip" on the throttle pedal to bring the engine speed up to 5000rpm. Now engine and transmission are all turning at matching speeds and as you let the clutch out everything will mesh together smoothly with no jerkiness at all.

To accomplish the same maneuver with a nonsynchromesh gearbox requires a little more concentration, but once mastered will give you a feeling of satisfaction every time you do it correctly.

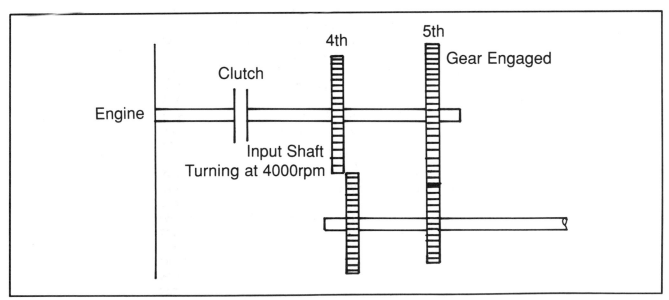

Fifth gear engaged with the input shaft turning at 4000rpm.

With a synchromesh gearbox the cones slide ahead of the gears so that when the gears arrive, the input and output shafts are already turning at matched speeds and the gears can mesh smoothly together. Without the synchromesh cones, you have to add a couple of steps in the middle of the operation and take some positive action to get the input shaft turning at the correct speed.

Look at the diagrams again. You are driving along in fifth gear at 4000rpm. This time when you push the clutch pedal in and move the gear lever, it is impossible for the gears to mesh correctly since the input shaft must be turning at 5000rpm before the fourth gear cluster engages. In order to obtain that speeding up of the input shaft, you must do it with the engine.

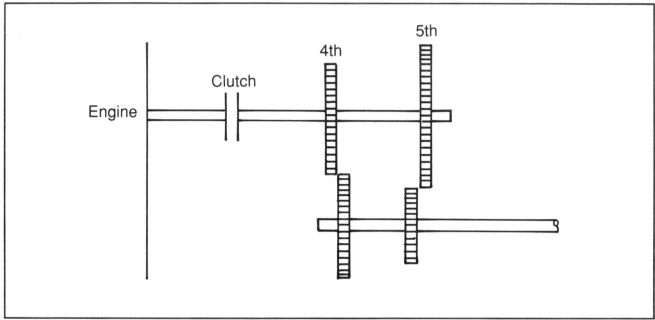

The gears in neutral while the clutch is out and the throttle is blipped to bring the input shaft up to 5000rpm.

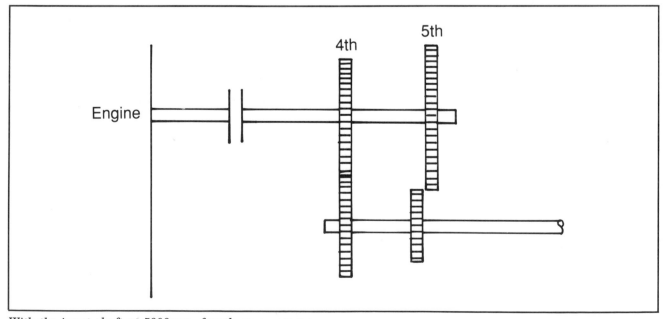

With the input shaft at 5000rpm, fourth gear engages cleanly.

The sequence without synchromesh is as follows:

1. Clutch in, foot off the throttle, and gear lever to neutral.

2. Clutch out (i.e., foot off the clutch pedal) so that the input shaft is turning at the same speed as the engine again.

3. "Blip" the throttle to bring the engine and the input shaft up to 5000rpm (or a little over).

4. Clutch in, gear lever to fourth gear.

5. Clutch out, foot back on the throttle pedal.

Braking While Downshifting

Assume you are on the main straight of a racetrack, traveling at about 150mph in fifth gear. The corner you are approaching has to be taken at about 40mph in second gear.

At point 'A' you start to brake as hard as possible. By the time you reach 'B' you are within the speed range for fourth gear, so you must come off the brake, execute a smooth double declutch gear change, and then go back to maximum braking again. You are now at 'BB.' When you reach 'C' you must repeat the operation in order to take third gear, getting back on the brakes again at 'CC.' One more time between 'D' and 'DD,' a little more braking, and you arrive at 'E,' where you turn into the corner.

The only problem is that, from a performance point of view, all the time spent between 'B' and 'BB,' 'C' and 'CC,' and 'D' and 'DD' was time wasted. Since you had to release the brakes during those periods in order to get the gear changing done, they were periods when you were not braking.

If the first gear change at point 'B' took place at 120mph, the second at point 'C' at 90mph, and the third at point 'D' at 60mph, and if each gear change took one second to execute, you will have traveled no less than 396ft during the gear-changing operations without braking!

Suppose you could *continue braking* while you did the double declutch gear shifting. You could go 396ft closer to the corner before putting on the brakes. At 150mph it takes 1.8 seconds to travel 396ft, so on just one corner of the racetrack you could save 1.8 seconds by braking to the limit *and* double declutch gear changing at the same time! Well, you can if you use heel-and-toe gearshifting.

Heel-and-Toe Gearshifting

The name heel-and-toe is actually a misnomer. You do not use either heel or toe! But whoever first discovered this procedure most certainly did.

Today all manual transmission cars have the pedals arranged the same way: clutch on the left, brake in the middle, and throttle on the right. But it wasn't always that way. I remember when I was first allowed (or sometimes not allowed, but I got there anyway) behind the wheel of the family car, which was a 1934 two-seater Morris 8 convertible with two "dickey" seats in the trunk. The clutch pedal was on the left, the brake pedal on the right, and the throttle pedal in the middle! Then drivers really did use heel and toe to cover both pedals at once.

Let's go back a few pages to where you were approaching a corner on the racetrack at 150mph. Because you won't lose time while changing gears, the reference points will now be A1, B1, and so on *(see diagram on page 117)*.

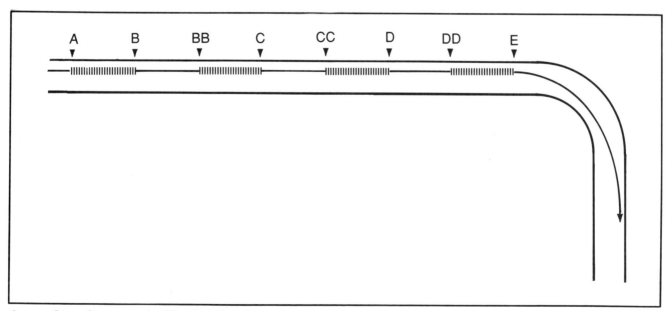

Approaching the corner, braking is only taking place at the shaded lines.

Today's pedal layout. This is a completely adjustable replacement pedal assembly.

This is how the pedals used to be arranged, clutch on the left, brake pedal on the right...and throttle pedal in the middle.

At 'A1' you apply the brakes. At 'B1' you do not release the brakes but continue to brake while doing the double declutch gear change above.

"Not possible," you say. "There are three pedals and I only have two feet!"

Remember in chapter 1 I talked about the possibility of doing some "minor surgery" to the pedals, and I said don't rush out and do it until you

...They are in this Mercedes, now owned by George F. Wingard, which won the French Grand Prix in 1914.

100

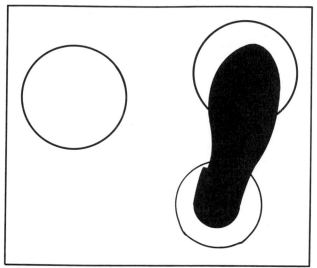

In the olden days, with pedals like these it really was heel and toe shifting.

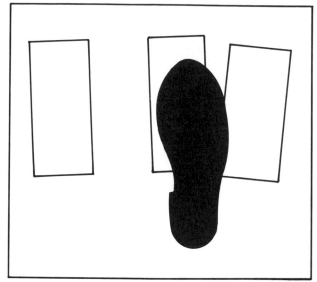

Today, it is actually a ballet dance on the toes.

have read chapter 8? Now is the time to do "it." In addition to putting blocks on the pedals, you should also enlarge the pedal area or approach the pedal surfaces relative to each other if necessary, so that when the right foot is hard on the brake pedal, you can still rotate it and "blip" the throttle with the right edge of the foot.

You can see that the braking will be done with the ball of the foot while the right edge of the foot, probably just behind the little toe, can still reach the throttle pedal.

Let's go back to point 'B1' above, where with the ball of the foot still hard on the brake pedal you make the first double declutch downshift. This time the "blip" is done with just the right edge of the right foot.

The sequence now becomes:

1. At 'A1,' foot on the brake, building up to the limit of threshold braking and keeping it there from now on.

2. At 'B1,' clutch in and gear lever to neutral.

3. Clutch out (i.e., foot off the clutch pedal) so that the input shaft is turning at the same speed as the engine again.

4. "Blip" the throttle to bring the engine and the input shaft up to 5000rpm. You do not need to look at the rev counter to do this, but you should learn to do it by sound and eventually just by feel alone.

5. Clutch in, gear lever to fourth gear.

6. Clutch out.

With constant braking throughout the maneuver you change down to third gear at 'C1,' to second gear at 'D1,' and at 'E' you are ready to turn into the corner. And you just gained a 1.8 second advantage in only one corner over your competitor who cannot do heel-and-toe gear changes!

Heel-and-Toe Shifting With Tiptronic

Many of you who now drive 911s or 968s with the Tiptronic transmission are probably wondering if you can apply the same technique. The answer is, yes, you can.

You already know that when changing up you can do so at full throttle with just a "tip" forward on the gear lever so that there is no lost time in acceleration. When you are changing down you will find that you can actually feel the electronic contact as you "tip" the gear lever backward. The "blip" should be done at precisely that moment to balance engine and transmission speeds. It might take a little time to develop the feel for that electronic contact because it is very delicate, but it is there.

Trail Braking

Remember that a tire can only do 100 percent of anything. If it is being used to provide 100 percent braking, it cannot steer. So if you are at absolute threshold braking in a straight line, you *cannot* steer the car. "Trail braking" is the term applied to gently trailing off the brakes as you increase steering into a corner.

If all the braking is done in a straight line, then at the turn-in point for a corner, no more braking is required. However, the first turning into a corner is very gradual and very transitional, so the turning effort required from the tires is relatively small.

Obviously things do not go along in 10 percent increments, but the diagram on page 118 will show you what I mean.

At the turn-in point for a corner, the steering effort required is perhaps 10 percent, which still leaves 90 percent of the tires' ability available for braking. The deeper the car goes into the corner, the more steering is required and, thus, the less is available from the tires for braking, which is allowed to "trail off." When you arrive at the "apex" of the corner (see chapter 9), you are using the steering to the maximum and you have no braking ability left. All the way from the turn-in point to the "apex" you reduce the braking as you increase the steering.

Antilock Braking System

Those of you who drive late-model Porsches as well as many other fine performance cars have ABS brakes, or the Antilock Braking System. This means that each wheel is equipped with a sensor device that recognizes when that wheel is about to lock up. It sends a message to the central computer, which then releases the pressure to the brake cylinder at that wheel. As soon as the wheel is rolling free again the brake fluid pressure is restored to the wheel.

On Porsches and most other high-performance cars, each wheel feeds information and is fed instructions independently, and each one can react up to fifteen times a second. So if you are driving with the two left wheels on dry asphalt and the two right ones in loose gravel at the edge of the road, the ABS might well be working on the right wheels but not on the left. But, at the limit of braking, each of the four would have the maximum grip available to it.

A tire can only do 100 percent of anything so if it is being used to provide 100 percent braking, it cannot steer. So if you are at absolute threshold braking in a straight line, you cannot steer the car.

The only disadvantage of ABS is the feeling generated beneath the foot and occasionally the noise that accompanies it (although on at least one expensive car on the market today, the Mercedes-Benz 500SL, even that has been engineered out of the system). Because the brake pressure at one or more wheels is constantly being released and restored, it feels as though the pedal is pushing back jerkily on the foot. At the same time, when the brakes and the ABS are working at the limit, you will hear the tires "chirping," and as you develop your sensitivity, you will actually feel the wheels

going round in little jerks as each one almost locks, is released, then almost locks again. Up to fifteen times a second!

At the time of writing there is a television commercial that suggests that nobody has feet that can move fast enough to beat an Antilock Braking System.

You remember I said that you probably have well-meaning but misinformed friends who have told you to use "cadence" braking? If you try to stab away at the brake pedal like that, then I agree, it is unlikely that you can stop shorter than the ABS. But with one exception, which I will discuss in chapter 11, stabbing away at the brake pedal is *not* the quickest way to slow down.

Getting to the ten level on the scale and holding it there is the quickest way to slow down. Holding the pressure at the ten level is done by controlling the pressure on the brake pedal, not by the number of times you stab at it. Since you control the pressure with the sensitivity in the ball of your foot, the number of adjustments you can make per second *is infinitely variable*. Clearly, a skilled driver can stop more quickly than a mechanical system that is limited to the number of times per second it can react.

A highly skilled driver can probably stop a car without ABS going at 60mph in the rain about 5ft shorter than the same car with ABS.

However, having said that, I acknowledge that the undeniable advantage of ABS is that anyone and everyone can use it to its maximum all the time. A highly skilled driver on a racetrack has all his or her concentration focused on driving the car. On the road it is wishful thinking to imagine that even that same driver applies the same amount of intense concentration to driving, and that is where ABS braking really comes into its own. With ABS, even with the brakes hard on, it is impossible to lock a wheel, so you can still steer around objects or out of trouble.

Left-Foot Braking

You saw in chapter 4 that front-wheel drive has certain advantages in normal transportation cars: Front-wheel-drive cars are cheaper to build, they allow more usable space within the vehicle, and they are inherently safe. However, from a performance point of view they leave much to be desired. As you know, a tire can only do 100 percent of something, and therein lies the weakness of front-wheel drive.

With a weight bias over the front wheels, while braking, and especially while trail braking, the front tires are being asked to do much more work than those at the rear. You can easily overstep the very fine line between having the front tires working at 100 percent of their capability or asking them to do more than 100 percent of their steering and braking capability, and you will find yourself winding on more and more steering with less and less effect!

So how do you get a front-wheel-drive car around a racetrack quickly? If you are a rally driver, how do you get around slippery corners quickly?

It would be nice to say, "Easy. Just use your left foot on the brake." In fact you do have to use your left foot on the brake—but it isn't easy!

The first problem to overcome is the fact that if you are used to driving "conventionally," the right foot is used to sensitive operation of both throttle and brake pedal. The left foot, on the other hand, is used to rapidly pushing the clutch in and equally rapidly letting it out again after a gear change. When you brake to a stop at a red light, the left foot pushes the clutch in briskly just before you stop in order not to stall the engine. It is not used to sensitivity when it pushes.

When I first learned to use the left foot on the brake, it took me about three months before I got to the point where I could come smoothly to a stop. In my early attempts the car would slow down reasonably smoothly until just before actually stopping, whereupon my left foot would suddenly think it was on the clutch, as usual, and would give a hefty shove, locking up the wheels with a screech and sending the occupants flying toward the windshield!

So, if you decide to learn left-foot braking, first *make sure everyone is wearing a seatbelt*, and practice when there is no other vehicle near you.

In a spin, both feet in! Left foot "in" on the clutch, right foot "in" hard on the brakes.

Left-Foot Braking with Front-Wheel Drive

Once you have mastered the technique of slowing down and stopping, you can go on to the next phase: using left-foot braking to help you around corners in a front-wheel-drive car.

In the situations mentioned above, overstepping the slip angles and the front tire ability will lead to violent understeer, and the car will want to go straight on. The inherent "negative safety" of front-wheel drive will come into play as you lift off the throttle pedal.

To overcome this negative safety and create a positive reaction from a front-wheel-drive car, you

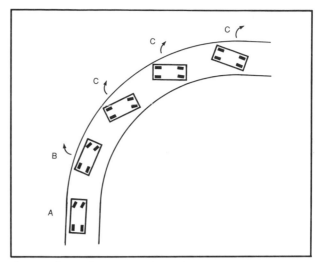

Approaching the corner at high speed, by 'B' you steer hard into the corner and jab the left foot on the brake while keeping the right foot hard on the gas. By 'C,' the car's tail will slide out and rotate.

must approach the corner *too fast,* so that doing nothing except lifting off the throttle and turning the steering wheel, would result in the car understeering off the road. At a speed too fast for the corner, turn in as usual and the car will start to understeer. At this point, while keeping your right foot hard on the gas pedal, you must start a series of "stabs" with the left foot on the brake pedal. Because the right foot is keeping the power on, these "stabs" will not lock the front wheels, but they will lock the rear ones. Losing traction, the rear wheels will immediately start to slide out toward the outside of the corner, which rotates the car and points it in the direction you want to go. With practice—a lot of practice—you will be able to judge at what speed you can enter any given corner and just how to "stab" your way around it.

One of the most famous of the "Flying Finns" was Timo Makinen, who was especially renowned for his exploits in the front-wheel-drive Mini Cooper. On one occasion at a press conference, he was asked how long it took to learn this advanced technique of left-foot braking. Timo's English, while adequate, was not brilliant, and after thinking for a moment, he replied, "It take at least two years and many, many cars!"

So for the budding front-wheel-drive car rally drivers amongst you, be warned. Try to have a supply of "many cars" to fall back on.

Left-foot braking can be used to advantage in most cars under certain conditions, and I will look at that in detail in chapter 11.

103

Chapter 9

Cornering

The place: Daytona International Speedway
The time: 1971, 11:45p.m., Saturday night
The occasion: The 24 Hours of Daytona

My first ever visit to the United States had been three years earlier. Having just won the 1968 Monte Carlo Rally, I got on a series of planes

Porsche 907, Daytona, 1968
Over the line in the long-tail 907 number 54 for victory in the Daytona 24 Hours on my first ever visit to the United States. Dave Friedman

Porsche 907, Daytona, 1968
*My winning car at speed on the tri-oval in the 1968 24
Hours of Daytona.* Dave Friedman

the next day, from Nice to Paris to New York to
Daytona Beach. Being so excited at winning the
"Monte," it was not until I got there and looked at
a map that I even knew where Daytona was!

*The larger the radius of a corner,
the faster you can drive around it.
Or, conversely, the faster you are
going, the larger the radius must be
in order to negotiate a corner safely.*

Then I won the 24 Hours in a Porsche 907—
Porsche's first in a twenty-four hour race and the
first of what was to be an incredible eighteen victories for Porsche over the next twenty-four years.

Even the best don't get it right all the time,
and 1969 saw the retirement of all five factory
Porsches with numerous exhaust and transmission problems. My codriver, Brian Redman, had an
even more bizarre incident. Driving through the
flat-out left turn in the infield in the middle of the
night, the fire extinguisher went off on its own ac-
cord. Blinded by the vapor and groggy from the gas
it gave off, poor Brian went off the road and got
thoroughly stuck in the mud. Because outside assistance was forbidden, he first had to get the

tears out of his eyes and then get some fresh air back in his lungs before eventually getting unstuck and making it back to the pits!

To corner comfortably at the limit of the car—and more particularly at the limit of the tires—you have to have balance.

The 1970 race wasn't much better. Although Kurt Ahrens and I stayed in contention with the Gulf-Wyer cars well into the night, Kurt had a rear tire puncture just after passing the pits, which meant he had to do almost a whole lap with the body dragging on the ground. Unfortunately, it wasn't just the body but the fuel tank as well, and by the time he made it back to the pits there was a sizable hole out of which the fuel was leaking—taking all our hopes with it.

With Gijs Van Lennep as my codriver in the Martini Racing 917, I had the pole position for the start of the 1971 race. Mark Donohue was along-

Daytona, 1968
Fortunately Daytona provided an outsize winners' garland! I shared the victory with Jochen Neerpasch, Rolf Stommelen, Jo Siffert and Hans Hermann. Dave Friedman

side me in the beautifully prepared Penske Ferrari 512. Pedro and Jo, of course, in the Gulf-Wyer 917s, were lined up side by side in the second row.

With a rolling start, the driver in pole position has the luxury of controlling the speed at the start of the race, and by now I knew enough about the performance characteristics of the Porsche 917 and the Ferrari 512 to make sure that the speed and the gear we were in across the start line was perfect for the Porsches and less than ideal for the Ferrari. As the green flag waved, I jumped into the lead, taking Jo and Pedro with me. They streamed down the inside into Turn 1 so close behind me that Mark had nowhere to go and was elbowed back into fourth place. Jo Bonnier in a Lola T70 was also in the hunt up front and the race settled down into a five-car battle.

One of the problems with 24 Hours at Daytona, compared to Le Mans, is that the driver is al-

Daytona, 1969
Brian Redman and I looking worried at Daytona in 1969. Vic Elford collection

Porsche 917, Daytona, 1970
The Porsche Austria 917 at Daytona in 1970. Leonard Turner

ways busy. At Le Mans, there is plenty of time to relax. Although it may sound incredible to the uninitiated, all the way down the Mulsanne straight at Le Mans, even at 240mph, the driver has little to do except keep the car pointing straight and check that all is well with the instruments. From the Mulsanne corner to Indianapolis, although the car is accelerating all the way, there is still not much to do, and from Arnage back to the White House, or now to the Porsche Curve, the same situation exists: no physical effort, and depending on traffic, not much mental effort either.

But at Daytona the driver is busy all the time. Even down the back straight (there was no chicane in those days), although physically you can relax, mentally you are preparing yourself for the entry to the east, banking flat out at 220mph. And no matter how many times you have already done it, you still have to convince yourself each lap that it is possible, especially at night. If there is traffic in front as you approach, it is even more difficult psychologically: you are wondering if the slower driver has seen you coming, wondering if he or she will stay low so that you can take the high line, trying to recognize the car—and even the driver's helmet—and trying to remember what that driver did last time you came up behind.

Shades of our little red Italian car at Sebring.

Porsche 917, Daytona, 1970
The 917 with Kurt Ahrens at the wheel, leading Jean-Pierre Beltoise in a Matra. Note the "skylight" above Kurt's head, specially built into the roof for Daytona so that the drivers could see further ahead round the banking. Dave Friedman

Porsche 917, Daytona, 1970
Heading into the night at Daytona. Dave Friedman

Porsche 917, Daytona, 1971
*The driver is very busy at Daytona. Here I squeeze the
917 through a pack of GT cars while one of the Ferrari
512s tries desperately to stay in touch.* Dave Friedman

It is also difficult to set up the car for Daytona because of the mixture of the banking and the flat, infield road section.

A couple of years earlier, Jo Siffert and I had done some testing at Daytona and we discovered an interesting fact: The time spent on the nearly 2.5 miles of the oval was almost identical to the time spent on the 1.2 miles of infield road. Because of the very high speed on the banking, the cars were always set up to understeer fairly heavily, which made them very difficult to drive on the infield. Jo and I reasoned that there was perhaps room to improve the overall lap time if we could negotiate the infield quicker, so we set up the car to handle better around the slower corners.

Then we went out and tried it. And we both came back after a lap or two white faced! By taking out some of the built-in understeer, the car would not stay down in the groove and we found the tail coming out and oversteering, in other words getting sideways, at 220mph on the banking. Needless to say, we rapidly put the car back to its original setup and just made do the best we could around the infield!

Now, fifteen minutes before midnight, attrition had already started to take its toll. Many cars were already parked in the garage, many drivers were already in bed back at their hotels, and traffic was light. Gijs and I were in a comfortable second place behind Jo Siffert and Brian Redman's

Porsche 917, Daytona, 1971
Long-distance endurance racing requires great team work. Here the Martini & Rossi Racing Team mechanics

go to work during a routine pit stop at night. Werkfoto Porsche

Gulf-Wyer car. As I built up speed on the back straight no one was in front of me, just the 31-degree banking in the distance, which I sensed rather than saw in the headlights. Having learned from some of the stock car drivers when I did the Daytona 500 a couple of years earlier, I used to dive in low and then let the car drift up almost to the wall.

This time, as I neared the wall, all hell broke loose. With no warning the car was suddenly spin-

Porsche 917, Daytona, 1971
Here I am side by side with Jo Siffert on the Daytona banking at 220mph. Although motor racing is probably *the fiercest of all competitive sports, drivers need to have absolute trust and respect for each other.* Dave Friedman

Porsche 917, Daytona, 1971
Here I come slicing through traffic on the infield. Werkfoto Porsche

ning and I was thankful for my couple of stock car races and particularly the advice offered by Richard Petty. At my first 500-mile "rookie" drivers meeting he had said, "If you get into a spin on the banking, turn left and put your foot hard on the brake. The car will continue to spin, but gravity will take over and it will slowly come down to the grass at the bottom of the banking." He added that "You can also close your eyes, but that is optional!"

I turned left, stood hard on the brake, but was much too fascinated (or frightened) to close my eyes. After what seemed like every couple of seconds, but was probably much more frequent than that, I would see the wall flash past in the headlights and then blackness again. After spinning like that for over 400 yards, the car finally came to a stop down on the infield grass. I breathed a sigh of relief and said a big "Thank you" to Richard Petty.

Porsche 917s were made to go very fast—forward but not backward—and the car had been ab-

solutely decimated by spinning at such high speed. The first time around the entire rear deck had been blown off; the second time, one of the doors had gone; the third time, the other door; and somewhere in between, the entire right rear corner, suspension, brake, and transmission had also parted company with the chassis.

As soon as the car stopped, my first thought was to get out and run—run from the possibility of another car doing the same thing and taking aim at me. But disoriented in the pitch black night, I had no idea where I was or which direction to run!

A few seconds later my dilemma was solved as a Porsche 911 erupted out of the night, followed closely by Mark Donohue's 512. As they transitioned onto the banking, both were blinded by the dust I had left behind. They touched, turning Mark into the wall and sending the 911 spinning out of control toward me. Now I knew which way to run and wasted no time getting under way.

The 911 hit what was left of the right rear corner of my car where I had been standing only seconds before and then launched itself into the air, coming to rest upside down a few yards away from where I now stood. I was the first on the scene to make sure the driver was OK and was quickly doubled over with mirth as the safety workers, with much shouting back and forth, searched unsuccessfully for the driver of the 917!

Talking with the Porsche engineers afterward, I discovered that I had been the victim of a failed safety device on the right rear wheel. For some time, the designers of Formula 1 and powerful prototype sports cars had been concerned with the possible consequences of a tire being dragged off the wheel rim by the centrifugal force generated by the G loading in corners, due to the high downforce we were now using.

Two systems were in the embryo stage of development to combat the problem. One, used primarily in Formula 1, actually had bolts inserted through the rim of the wheel after the tire was mounted, so that the tire could not slide inward on the rim. Porsche was experimenting with another system, where the rim had a beading about an eighth of an inch high running all the way around the inside of the rim, so that once mounted correctly the tire could not slide inward.

Alfa Romeo Tipo 33/3TT, Daytona, 1972
After the 917s were outlawed at the end of 1971, I moved to Alfa Romeo. Although the Italian "joie de vivre" made life fun, it lacked the Porsche precision to win races. Here I am at the wheel of the Alfa Romeo Tipo 33/3TT at Daytona. Bill Warner

Unfortunately, the right rear wheel on my car, which around the banking of Daytona is the one subjected to the highest centrifugal force, had a flaw in the beading. In fact, the beading was breaking up, and after, presumably, a number of laps with the tire trying to force its way past the bead, it broke up completely, allowing the tire to slip inward to the tire well in the center of the wheel.

At that point there was no longer any tire adhesion to the road and the car went into an instantaneous spin. From there on I was just a passenger, with no control and even little comprehension of what was happening.

Those of you who follow motor racing on television are probably wondering how I can make such an admission. After all, you have heard some—and I emphasize the *"some"*—commentators who, with a greater sense of the dramatic than reality, frequently tell you that so-and-so has just marvelously controlled a spin at 180mph. Such a commentary is absolutely absurd. A driver might react and do the right thing, but to suggest that he or she has control of the events is pure nonsense. In fact, I believe that I have heard Rick Mears, perhaps the greatest IndyCar driver of all time, quoted as saying a similar thing. There is a speed, which probably varies from driver to driver but which I would guess, at least in my case, is generally at around 150mph, beyond which the driver's brain can no longer keep up with events as they happen. Not only do you have no control over what is happening, but you are constantly one step behind even understanding what is happening.

The Importance of Cornering

As I said earlier, incredible though it might seem, driving down the Mulsanne straight at Le Mans at 240mph, even at night, is actually quite relaxing. Almost too relaxing, in fact, since it gives the driver time to think about all the possible consequences if something were to go wrong or if some vital part were to break! But apart from that, there is no great skill required to go fast in a straight line. Anyone can do it.

Going around corners, however, is something else. Between driving in an absolutely straight line and driving around a tight corner, many different forces come into play concerning your car and your driving technique.

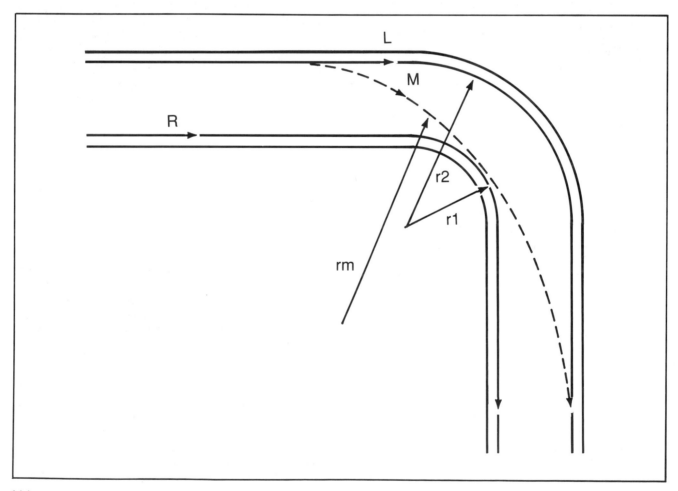

Cooper F1, French Grand Prix, 1968
Perfect cornering balance as I take my Cooper to fourth place in a wet French Grand Prix. Not bad for my first Formula 1 race! Vic Elford collection

Speed and Cornering

Some years ago, the great pre- and postwar Italian Grand Prix driver Piero Taruffi came up with a formula that explained how fast a car could go in any given circumstance. By eliminating all the known constants from the equation, it boils down to simply the larger the radius of a corner, the faster you can drive around it. Or, conversely, the faster you are going, the larger the radius must be in order to negotiate a corner safely.

Let's look at a typical corner again in the diagram. There are many ways you could drive around the corner. You could just stay on the right and follow the 'R' path. You could stay left and follow the 'L' path. The *radius* of the corner will be 'r1' or 'r2' depending on which you choose.

But from the formula above, you know that the *larger* the radius the faster you can go. Or, if you are not interested in speed, the larger the radius, the less stress you place on the car and there-

fore the *safer* it will be for a given speed. So if you take the line 'M,' you will have the largest possible radius, 'rm,' through the corner and therefore the fastest. Or the least stressful on the car if you are driving at a predetermined speed.

Although this applies primarily to the racetrack, the same theory can also be used on the road. You just have to remember that there might be someone coming in the opposite direction, so be careful to use only your half of the road, and don't go wandering over the yellow line!

Balance and Cornering

Cornering, you might think, is really quite simple. Slow the car down, turn the steering wheel, and the car will go round the corner.

That is one way, but put as simply as that, it means that you are making the front tires do all the work in getting you around the corner. The faster you go using that basic technique, the more

115

you will load the front tires, until eventually they will be screaming at you.

To corner comfortably at the limit of the car—and more particularly at the limit of the tires—you have to go all the way back to balance, which I discussed in chapter 2. Because a tire can only do 100 percent of something, if you can help the front tires by using the *balance* of the car to help it rotate, you should also get through the corner more quickly and comfortably.

Let's refer back to chapter 8. You are approaching the same corner at 150mph in fifth gear, but the corner can only be taken in second gear at 40mph. From 'A1' all the way to 'D1' you were braking and downshifting using the heel-and-toe technique. From 'D1' onward, you were still braking, preparing for the crucial point, 'E,' where you start to turn, still trail braking, into the corner.

The car is turning more and more sharply as it approaches the apex of the corner and the brakes

Porsche 908/3, Nürburgring, 1971
Balance and concentration helped me to my third Nürburgring 1000km victory, this time in the Martini Racing Team Porsche 908/3. Werkfoto Porsche

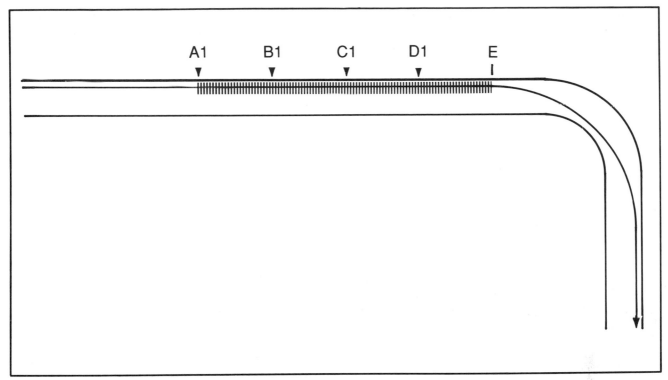

Braking without interruption from 'A1' to 'E.'

are trailing off. What you do now, at the apex of the corner, will determine your speed through that part of the corner and especially your speed *out* of the corner.

If you are like most people, you take your foot off the brake, jam it down on the throttle pedal, wrench the wheel around more, and start powering out of the corner, at which point you will be asking the front tires to do much more than the 100 percent they are capable of!

By delicately changing the balance of the car during the entire cornering operation you can help rotate the car by persuasion rather than force.

Right at the apex is when you need maximum steering ability, but jamming your foot down on the throttle pedal will give an instant weight transfer to the rear wheels and will take away a lot of the front wheels' ability to steer. The harder you accelerate, the more steering you will have to wind on and the less effect the steering will have

because the weight transfer leaves the front wheels with less and less grip. The car will start understeering, the front wheels will be literally "pushing" toward the outside of the corner, and the front tires will start screaming—for help!

By delicately changing the balance of the car during the entire cornering operation you can help rotate the car by persuasion rather than force.

As you approach 'E,' the front tires will be fully loaded and using 100 percent of their ability in braking. At 'E' the brakes will start to trail off and the steering will start to be applied. If you come smoothly off with the brakes and smoothly on with the steering all the way to the apex, the last adjustment to balance will be made.

At the instant that you release the brakes completely a last transfer of weight toward the rear wheels will occur. During this weight transfer, there will be a moment when the front tires have maximum steering ability and at that point you will actually feel the car rotate around the apex. Now, remember the piece of string around the big toe discussed in chapter 7? Once the car has rotated, you can gently apply power as the steering wheel unwinds until you reach maximum power as the front wheels arrive at the straight-ahead position.

You can gain a better understanding of the dynamics of what is happening and a comprehension of what I will call "the 100 percent tire rule"

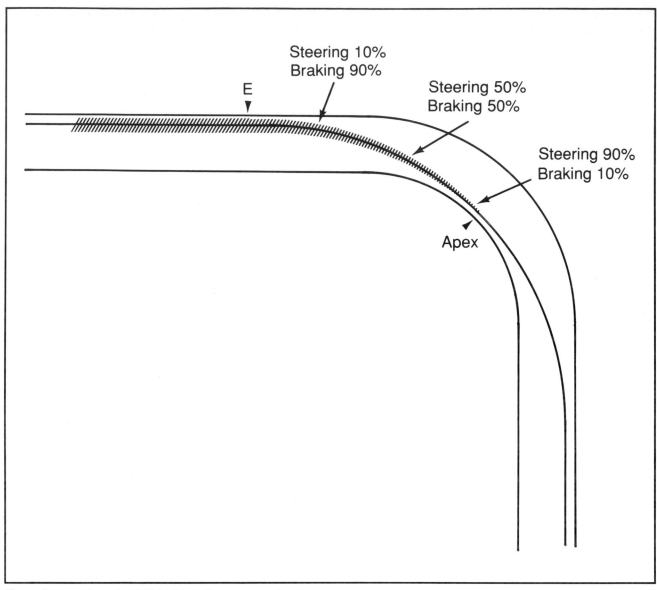

Steering 10%
Braking 90%

Steering 50%
Braking 50%

Steering 90%
Braking 10%

E

Apex

From the turn-in point 'E,' braking decreases or "trails off" as steering input increases.

through a simple graphical description known as the friction circle.

If you tie a string to your rearview mirror and hang a heavy metal ball (or other object) on the other end, what will happen when you exert a force on it?

When you are braking heavily, the ball will swing toward the front of the car. Accelerating will make it swing toward the rear. Turn left and it will go to the right; turn right and it will swing left. If you combine braking and turning, as in trail braking into a corner, it will swing both forward and sideways and lean toward one front corner of the car. As you accelerate and unwind out of a corner, it will swing back and sideways.

In the diagram, you can see that when maximum braking is being used in a straight line, the position of the braking force is at 'Bm.' As both trail braking and steering are applied for a left turn, the amount of braking moves back to position 'B1,' and if the maximum use is being made of the tires, the steering input will be at 'L1.' The resultant force will be at position '1.' Further into the corner the braking will be at 'B2' and the steering at 'L2,' giving a resultant at '2.'

Similarly, exiting a right turn just after the apex, the steering effort will be at 'R1,' allowing acceleration to be at 'A1.' Further out of the corner and acceleration will have increased to 'A2' as steering diminishes to 'R2.' When the car is finally totally straight again, the reading on the 'R' scale will be zero and on the 'A' scale it will be 'Am.'

If you are using the tires to their maximum ability at 100 percent and were to plot the friction resultants an infinite number of times, you would finish up with a perfect circle joining the infinite number of dots. Anything less than 100 percent, whether it be on braking or acceleration or in the cornering force applied, will give a resultant somewhere inside the friction circle. In actual fact, it will not be an exact circle but slightly elliptical as tires can generate more G force under braking or acceleration than in a corner.

No matter what car you are driving, under reasonable road conditions, this technique does not change. Even in the wet, the procedure is the same, but you must develop a very sensitive touch and feel for what the car is doing in order to go quickly.

In a car with high downforce, such as a Formula 1, IndyCar, or Sports Prototype racer, it is true that you need a fair amount of pure physical force to drive it. But the Porsche you drive on the street needs little force, just balance.

In a car with high downforce, such as a Formula 1, IndyCar, or Sports Prototype racer, it is true that you need a fair amount of pure physical force to drive it. But the Porsche you drive on the street needs little force, just balance.

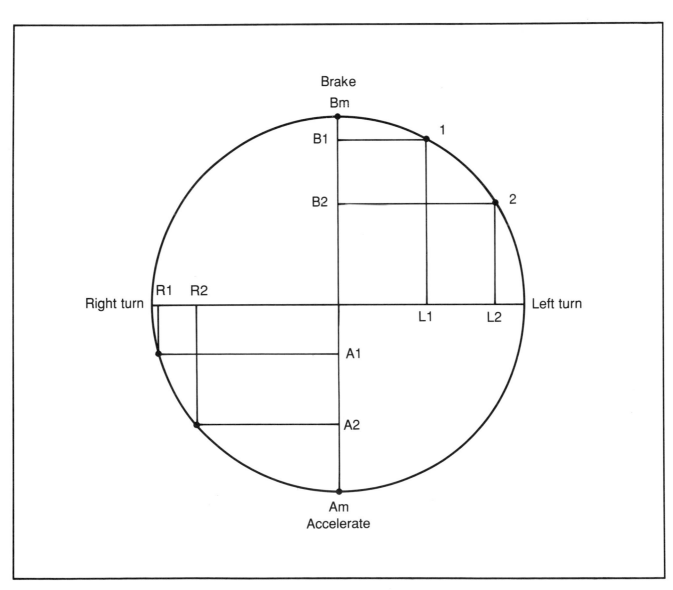

In 1976, I was the team manager for the French Inaltera sports car team. Inaltera was a manufacturer of high-quality and expensive wall coverings and had decided to invest in a brand new two-car team for the 24 Hours of Le Mans. The attempt was a success and with Inaltera about to expand into the American market, we also came to the 24 Hours of Daytona in 1977. Although from a racing point of view we went away empty-handed with neither car finishing, from a commercial point of view the company was delighted with the results. Because such a high percentage of racing fans in the United States are women, who, of course, have a lot to say in the buying of products like wall coverings, we decided that one of the Inalteras at Daytona would be driven by an all-female crew: Christine Beckers from Belgium and Lella Lombardi from Italy. Lella, incidentally, was and still is the only woman ever to score a point—or a half point to be exact as the race was stopped because of rain—in a Formula 1 world championship event.

The Daytona organizer, the late Bill France, Sr., loved the extra exposure that such a team gave to the race and when both the women expressed an interest in stock cars, he invited then back for the Firecracker 400 in July.

Neither Christine nor Lella were amazons; I doubt that either of them were more than about 5ft tall and 100lbs in weight, and both were looked upon with a certain amount of awe in the NASCAR garage area.

At a press conference a couple of days before the race, Lella was asked how in the world an itsy bitsy little girl like her was going to compete with all the big husky male drivers in two ton stock cars. She replied, "But I only have to drive the car, not carry it," and even the most chauvinistic reporters were rolling on the floor in laughter.

The fact that both were able to run at a very competitive speed in the race underlines the fact that balance is of far greater value in driving well than brute force.

Chapter 10

Sliding, Skidding, and The Art of Car Control

The place: Sweden
The time: A cold, cold winter in 1967
The occasion: The Swedish Rally

I had been to Sweden for the Swedish Rally in 1966 in a Ford Lotus Cortina. Remember, Ford gave me a practice car with no heater!

Porsche 911, Swedish Rally, 1967
My beautiful 911 ready for the start of a very cold
Swedish Rally. Lars-Olof M. Gnil

This time, David Stone and I had been able to practice in a civilized car lent to us by the Porsche importer. It even had the additional gasoline-fired, cold weather package, supplementary heater. Those of you who have owned older Porsche 911s with the heavy-duty cold weather package will remember that little heater. For those of you who do not, it had its own little compartment tucked away under the carpeting of the front luggage trunk.

The best way to control skids is not to have them in the first place.

If the heater was not there, the compartment was just empty and apparently served no useful purpose. A few years later I was to find that some people had presumably discovered a practical, if rather less than legal use for it.

(In 1970, I left England to make my home in France in the little town of Annemasse, just over the border from Geneva, Switzerland. For shopping, visiting friends, or simply going to lunch or dinner, I used to cross the border almost daily and sometimes even two or three times a day. I was soon on quite friendly terms with all the French customs officers, who would usually recognize me and the car and just wave me through.

(One day, however, a customs officer that I knew well pulled me out of line and started asking questions about where I had been and what I had been doing in Switzerland, all the time casually looking around inside the car. He suddenly asked me to open the front hood, pulled aside the carpet and went straight for the auxiliary heater compartment. I told him that the car did not have the extra heater, and he replied that it wasn't the heater he was looking for, "but you would be amazed what we find in there sometimes!")

But back to Sweden...and the cold.

Porsche 911, Swedish Rally, 1967
A typical special stage on the Swedish Rally. Lars-Olof M. Gnil

122

Porsche 911, Swedish Rally, 1967
Ice racing on the Swedish Rally. Lars-Olof M Gnil

Most championship rallies usually announced the route of the event well in advance, so that crews could make "pace notes" and practice. In Sweden the route was kept secret until the start, so practicing was limited to (in our case) simply learning more and more about driving on snow and ice. And there is probably no better place in the world to learn about sliding, skidding, and the art of car control than Sweden in winter.

While the country has a superb network of main highways connecting the major population centers, the vast majority of its road system is made up of well-graded gravel roads that twist and turn up and down through the eternal forest. It is on these little roads, covered in snow, that the rally takes place.

Just to make things even more interesting, the organizers invariably come up with some "against the clock" special stages that would be impossible anywhere else.

How about four-lap races, four cars at a time, around a one mile, flat, horse racing oval track? There may be as much as 4ft of snow on the ground, but they plow the racing surface and then send a street cleaning truck out to water it down so the surface is pure ice. Then they run the races at night, with as many as 50,000 people sitting in the grandstands cheering on their favorites!

Or a forty mile special stage carved out at random by a snow plow on a frozen river? This stage had no less than three passages underneath a large bridge so that the spectators on the bridge could get as much opportunity as possible to see the drivers at work!

Depending on the terrain, you can usually get a feeling for where a road is going to go next, even in a forest. But when the "road" is carved out of 4ft thick snow on a frozen river, it is impossible to see where it goes and equally impossible to anticipate.

Driving in those conditions is one long slide, so it is important to learn how to control that slide.

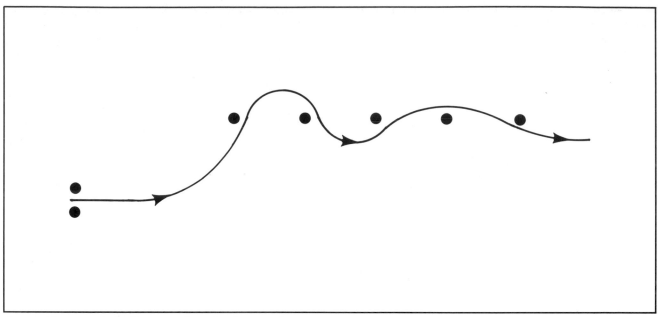

Start wide around the first cone then slowly smooth out and straighten the line as you go through the five cones.

The whole process of regaining control from a skid is described by the acronym CPR, which stands for Control, Pause, and Recovery.

Avoiding Skids and Slides

Of course, the best way to control skids is not to have them in the first place. To avoid skidding when road conditions are bad, every movement or action must be done using almost excessive smoothness. You must bring to bear everything you have learned from the previous pages about smoothness, balance, transitions, and anticipation so that you have no surprises.

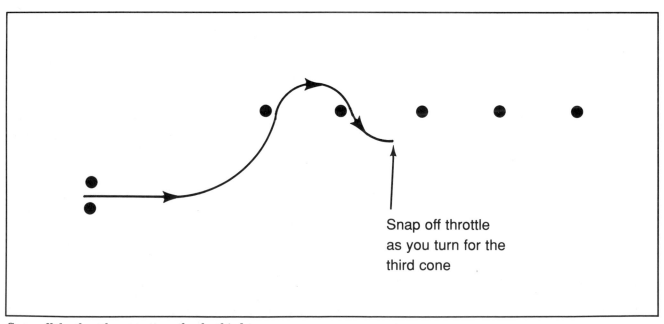

Snap off throttle as you turn for the third cone

Snap off the throttle as you turn for the third cone.

Hurried or jerky reactions usually happen when something takes you by surprise, so being constantly *ahead* of what is happening will help you avoid that unpleasant feeling of not knowing what's coming next.

Unfortunately, in the real world, skidding or sliding is going to happen eventually, so time spent learning what to do about it is a good investment. Stamping on the brakes on a slippery road is a sure way to create a skid, either with the wheels locked and the car sliding straight on, or with the car spinning if you're turning a corner. However, once you become thoroughly confident with the threshold braking technique from chapter 9, skidding should not be a problem.

Apart from the brakes, the other thing that can get you into trouble and cause a skid, a slide, or even a spin is violent use of the throttle pedal. Trying to accelerate too hard in a corner can cause the rear wheels (in a rear-wheel-drive car) to lose adhesion and slide out from under you.

Trailing Throttle Oversteer

Lifting off the throttle in a corner can also cause the rear wheels to lose adhesion and slide. Once the car is set into a balanced mode and accelerating through a corner, snapping off the throttle will cause what is known as trailing throttle oversteer.

A good way to experience this and to practice control is to find a deserted, closed-off parking lot, buy yourself a few traffic cones, and set up a slalom exercise as shown. First, practice driving through the slalom at fixed speeds. Start at say 15mph, then increase to 20, then 25, and so on, doing a number of runs at each speed and moving on to the higher speed only when you are thoroughly comfortable. Then start the slalom at say 15–20mph and try to *steadily increase the speed* all the way through.

When you are comfortable with that, it's time to go on to the next exercise and *make* the car slide. Again, start into the slalom at 15–20mph and increase speed as you go. But this time, as you turn the wheel to go around the third traffic cone, snap off the throttle pedal completely.

What will happen?

Because snapping off the throttle gives an instant weight transfer to the front of the car, the front wheels suddenly have *more* grip to steer with and the rear wheels will suddenly have *less* grip and will slide outward. This is trailing throttle oversteer.

Regaining Control From a Skid

What do you do when the rear of the car slides outward?

You probably remember from drivers education in high school that you are supposed to steer in the direction of the skid. But you probably were not told much else, as though steering into the skid was some sort of magic remedy and everything would be all right. In fact, there is more to do than just steering into the skid—and some things *not* to do in order to regain control of the car.

The whole process is described by the acronym CPR. This is not the medical variety; in this case CPR stands for Control, Pause, and Recovery. Control is the first movement: steering into the direction of the skid. Pause is the waiting period while the car loads up the suspension and takes on a "set" position. Recovery is slowly unwinding the steering wheel as the car starts to go in a straight line again.

Those are the things you must do. What you *must not* do is touch the pedals. No clutch, no brake, and above all, no throttle. You must master the situation you have created for yourself with just the steering wheel and the balance of the car. Touching any of the pedals will only add further instability, making recovery almost impossible.

Back in chapter 4, I mentioned that one of the problems many drivers have is not moving quickly enough. In this exercise, the control movement must be almost a reflex and must be done virtually instantaneously. The pause will vary in length according to the car, the tires, and the surface conditions. The recovery must be, as is so often the case, a smooth, gentle transition back to the straight-ahead position.

Regaining Control From a Spin

With your first attempt at CPR it is quite likely that you will not react quickly enough and the car will start to spin. If this happens and you are reasonably sure that you are indeed beyond the point where you can regain control, keep in mind the saying that most racing schools use: *In a spin, both feet in!*

Left foot "in" on the clutch, right foot "in" hard on the brakes. By disengaging the clutch you will keep the engine running so that when the spin ends you will be able to drive away again. By locking up the brakes you ensure that the car will stop in the shortest possible distance. At the same time you also ensure that it keeps going straight, by which I mean, in the direction it was going when it started to spin.

Do not be tempted, as the speed is scrubbed off, to think that you can let off the brakes and have control again. Even at low speed, the combination of the car rotating and the fact that you will probably not know which direction the front wheels are pointing, could result in the car jerking dangerously to one side or the other if you let the brakes off. Wait until it has *totally* stopped before trying to drive off again.

This is particularly important on a racetrack.

On a flat surface, when the car is spinning with all four wheels locked, it will always keep going in a straight line, which means that drivers following you can take avoiding action and be reasonably sure that they are going to miss you! Thanks to my monumental spin at Daytona and Richard Petty's advice, I know that on a banked track a car will come down the banking while it spins, and it is also reasonably predictable for the drivers trying to miss the spinning car.

It is possible during your first attempts at CPR that you will overreact with the first control action but not get the pause right, in which case the rear end will swing rapidly and viciously back the other way. If that happens, you have almost certainly lost control of the car. Don't even *think* about trying to recover, just put both feet in as fast as possible and wait for it to stop. In fact, most road accidents involving skidding cars come as a result of overreacting to the first skid and then not knowing what to do next. Once the car starts to snap back the other way, it builds up kinetic energy so fast that even the best driver has little chance of regaining control.

The only problem with the above exercises is that if you drive a fairly recent Porsche on modern Goodyear Eagle or other high-performance tires on a dry surface, it will be extremely difficult to get the car to slide. If you can do the exercises on a wet day you will get better results. Otherwise, try to find an area with a dusty or sandy surface that will let the car slide more easily.

Front-Wheel-Drive Control

The CPR approach also works with front-wheel-drive cars. Although the weight distribution is different to start with, the dynamics are basically the same.

All-Wheel-Drive Control

With a four-wheel-drive car such as a Carrera 4, once the car has taken a set and started to recover, you can start to accelerate. But this time, steer *back into the corner* instead of into the skid, as the driven front wheels will now actually help to pull the car back into its desired turning arc.

Chapter 11

Driving in Unusual Conditions

**The place: The town of Elgon on the
Kenya/Uganda border
The time: 1964
The occasion: The East African Safari Rally**

My first trip to one of the most naturally beautiful countries in the world was destined to be full of action and surprises. It would also see me go home with some new physical scars.

Ford Cortina GT, East African Safari Rally, 1964
*First service point on the East African Safari Rally with
my Cortina GT along with Eric Carlsson's Saab. The*
*driver's nationality is always painted over the wind-
shield to help the spectators recognize their favorites.*
Ford of Britian

On only my second rally for Ford of Britain I was to drive a Cortina GT in the East African Safari and already things were not going quite the way they were planned. It was about midnight on the second day of the team reconaissance trip and our team manager, Bill Barnett, responded to a knock on his door. When he opened the door, Bill was treated to the sight of my codriver Leon Baillon and I, covered in mud and blood and bandages, standing forlornly in front of him!

We had a long story to tell. When I arrived in Nairobi my practice car was not ready. With my friend John Sprinzel, I whiled away the time around the hotel swimming pool, but even though the sky was overcast, the sun's penetration at that latitude, virtually on the equator, and at that altitude of about 5,000ft, sent me to bed with a touch of sunstroke.

With Bill in attendance to oversee the logistics, the rest of the team left to start driving over the route. Leon and I left Nairobi some thirty-six hours later, determined to drive day and night until we caught up with them.

We have already seen how important balance is in braking, steering, and accelerating. Another feature of understanding and controlling the balance of the car is the ability to lift the car over obstacles.

We were just thirty miles from their second overnight stop at Elgon when on a steep, downhill, heavily cambered right-hand bend leading to a small bridge, I lost control of the car at about 60mph, spun, rolled, and somersaulted over a river, and crashed upside down on the other side, onto a huge tree stump.

Remember the seatbelts from chapter 1? Well, Leon and I were groggy, we both had blood pouring down our faces, but we were still alive and still conscious.

A group of youths approached down the track, singing drunkenly after a night at the local bar, and I admit to being a little apprehensive at the possible outcome of their finding two apparently rich foreigners with their car upside down beside the road. Leon, who had previously lived in Kenya, told me not to speak and proceeded to negotiate in Swahili in order to get the car turned right side up again. After a quick check on the oil level to make sure it had not all drained out through the filler cap we were under way again. Leon drove, as

blood was coming from the region of my right eye, which was already swollen and closed, leaving me half blind.

Straight to the hospital we went and presented our sorry selves to the "emergency department." Remember, this was a hospital in Africa in the sixties! The only doctor/surgeon on duty had just finished performing a cesarean operation. He told us we would have to wait a few minutes as they were just cleaning up the operating room. Through the open door we could see attendants washing down walls, floor, and ceiling with a high-pressure garden hose!

A few minutes later, Leon and I were both overcome with an excess of politeness when the question was raised as to who should go first. My face and eyebrow were soon stitched up, but poor Leon, who had a deep gash in the middle of his scalp, was less lucky aesthetically. First they had to shave all the hair away, so when he was finished, he looked like a Mohican in reverse—no hair back to front down the middle of his head, but hair sprouting all around on either side.

That was the sight that confronted Bill Barnett when he opened the door of his hotel room.

The car, of course, was a total write-off, so after a few hours sleep, it was back to Nairobi for another one. But every cloud has a silver lining, and we were treated to a low-level two-hour flight to Nairobi in a little Cessna. We flew over a perpetually changing wildlife scene, the most impressive part being the thousands of pink flamingos on the shores of Lake Naivasha.

The Safari Rally was, and still is, unique in the world, in that although the cars are racing against the clock, the roads *are not closed to normal traffic!* In fact, that is less dangerous than one might expect, because since the first "Coronation Safari" (to mark the accession to the throne of England of Queen Elizabeth II in 1953), the rally has taken on a totally national aspect, involving originally all three East African countries and more recently, just Kenya. It is held during the weekend of Easter, everyone is on holiday, and virtually the entire population either stays at home or seeks out the ideal or the nearest spot (depending on their means) to watch the cars go by.

Normally Easter means the rainy season, but this year, as we left Nairobi, it was still dry. The first thirty-six hour leg of the rally would lead us northward into Uganda and then up into the wild North East frontier territory bordering on Ethiopia and Somalia. There our first real setback occurred when we broke a steering arm. Way out in this moonscape, I had to drive a hundred miles with steering on only one wheel! We made it to the next service point but the time lost dropped us way back in the field. Repairs were made and we started to slowly claw our way up again.

By the start of the second leg, the long-awaited rains had arrived—with a vengeance. As we drove into the night, what had been well-defined tracks just days earlier became unending lakes of water. At one point I came across the Ford team leader, Henry Taylor, hopelessly bogged down in a seemingly endless, muddy lake. I stopped, got out the tow rope, and dragged Henry to apparently solid ground where I became stuck myself. Whereupon Henry unhitched the tow rope with the words, "Well, of course, with your problems on the first day, you're out of it now, so I can't waste time helping you," and promptly drove off! Not all Englishmen are gentlemen...far from it. As so often happens in Africa, out of nowhere some potential pushers materialized and with Leon's knowledge of Swahili and the changing of hands of some shillings from our kitty of "push money" we were soon on our way.

The water had been so deep when we initially stopped, that just opening the doors had allowed it to flow through almost up to the level of the seats. Trying to dry out my shoes in those conditions was, of course, just an exercise in futility so I simply took them off and drove for the next thirty-six hours barefoot. While I would not recommend it for everyday driving, you would be amazed at the increased sensitivity you feel when there is not even a thin sole between your feet and the pedals.

Driving in Rain and Water

Driving in wet, muddy conditions like that is something of a challenge. First, you have no idea where the track is—if indeed there was one to start with—nor how deep the puddles are as you drive into them. If you are driving a front-engine car, with the radiator and cooling fan up front, you must be careful to balance the need for speed with the need to keep the engine dry and running.

Driving on ice and snow or on smooth graded gravel roads can be an immense source of pleasure— but you need a lot of practice to obtain proficiency.

You must keep the speed up so that in the event of the wheels getting into some particularly slippery slime you will have enough momentum to carry you through it. On the other hand, you must not just charge in blindly, as water is likely to come rushing through the radiator and then get sprayed all over the electrical system causing complete ignition failure. If that happens you have only one choice, open up the hood and completely dry the entire system, which, if it is still raining, is a lot easier said than done!

If you know in advance that you are likely to meet such conditions, it might pay to wrap all the electrical leads in silicon grease, or use a silicon spray to insulate them. The only problem with that treatment is that any moisture already inside the system will be trapped and could itself cause problems as it heats up and vaporizes and can't get out.

Another problem in torrential rain, particularly when the temperature is high, which happens frequently in Africa, is keeping the inside of the windshield clear. Today many proprietary products are on the market, although you probably won't find too many of them in parts of Africa. However, one of the most effective ways of keeping the windshield clear is just plain old household soap, the sort that your grandmother might have used to scrub the kitchen table many years ago. Just rub it all over the inside of the windshield with a damp cloth, let it dry thoroughly, and then, with a soft dry cloth, very, very gently, taking care not to smear it, polish it off.

Above all, when you are driving in the rain, make sure you do everything *smoothly*. Tire grip does go away in the rain, of course, but it goes away much less in a straight line than in cornering. You can still accelerate fairly quickly in the rain, and once you develop the feel for threshold braking, you can still stop quickly, but you must be very gentle in the corners.

Aquaplaning

For normal road or racetrack driving in the rain, you must be aware of "aquaplaning," or "hydroplaning" as it is sometimes called. This occurs when there are puddles on the road and the tire is unable to penetrate them to maintain contact with the road surface underneath. Then the tire is separated from the road and actually slides along a film of water between it and the road surface.

Under these conditions, there is absolutely nothing you can do until the tire eventually makes contact with the road again. To limit the possibility of losing control of the car, make sure that the front wheels are pointing straight ahead, so if you are turning, bring the wheel back straight. If you are accelerating or braking when it happens, get your feet off the pedals immediately and just sit and wait until the contact and the grip come back again.

One of the problems with aquaplaning is that it happens almost exclusively at fairly high speed, so unlike other conditions, where you can practice slowly and build up to speed, you have to be ready to act almost instinctively when it happens for the first time!

129

Porsche 917, Brand Hatch, 1970
*Here I am in a monumental drift in the Porsche Austria
917 in the rain at the 1970 Brands Hatch 6 Hours—and
no, I didn't spin! After driving for over 5 1/2 hours of the
6 Hour race in these conditions, I finished second. Eric
della Faille*

Off-Road Driving

Driving in any off-road conditions, whether it be the rough rocky tracks of East Africa on the Safari Rally, the treacherous sand dunes of the Sahara desert on the Paris-Dakar, or just weekend camping, hunting, and fun in the wilderness near your home, requires a little preparation.

First, of course, make sure the vehicle is in tip-top condition: all the fluids topped up, all the windows clean, and the tires at the correct pressure. If you are going away from civilization, take along some concentrated food substances such as chocolate or glucose for energy and plenty of water. Even in the Sahara desert you can live for quite a while without food—but you cannot live long without water! And even in the Sahara, it can freeze at night, so take some blankets for warmth as well. A hand-operated winch and an anchor spike, hammer, and a good length of high-test nylon rope might be worthwhile too. But don't fill the car to the brim with everything you can lay hands on. The biggest enemy of all when you get off road is *weight*.

In 1981 I had my first experience at the Paris-Dakar Rally at the wheel of a Russian Lada. Strange selection, you might think, but the choice was not mine. After numerous injuries and even deaths during the early running of the event, the organizers had teamed up with a group of French doctors called "Médicins sans Frontières" to provide mobile medical assistance during the rally itself. Half a dozen Lada 4x4s had been provided by the French importer for this purpose, and each was manned by an experienced driver and a doctor.

I volunteered to drive one of these medical assistance vehicles because it seemed like a good way to get practical experience of the rally while saving my own money and being useful at the same time. After covering the entire route, with a few side trips to deliver injured competitors to hospitals and air ambulances, I felt ready to go back and try to win.

But with what?

During its early days, virtually everyone entered the Paris-Dakar with what the Europeans call 4x4 "Jeep"-type vehicles: Range Rovers, Mercedes G Wagons, Toyotas, Ladas, and so on. Watching from the wheel of my "ambulance," I started to realize that for most competitors, the vehicles were their own worst enemies. Reinforcement of the chassis and heavy skid plates to protect the underside, for example, created a vicious circle. The more reinforcement they added, the heavier the vehicle, the greater the fuel consumption, and the more fuel and therefore weight they had to carry. And the more they suffered in the extreme conditions.

At some time in the late 1970s, I had read and been impressed by a road test report on the Subaru Hatchback 4x4. At that time I lived in a little village outside Brussels and I persuaded the Belgian importer to lend me one for a few days to get the feel of it. As it happened, I had the car during a particularly bad winter spell when the roads were covered in ice. The road in front of my house was on a fairly steep slope and I was immediately able to test the four-wheel-drive capabilities of the little car. From a standing start using only front-wheel drive, not only could I not get the car moving, it actually slid backward down the hill while the front wheels were vainly trying to get it moving up the hill! Engaging the four-wheel-drive system, I was able to simply drive away as though on a dry road. If the Subaru four-wheel-drive system worked like that on ice, it should be the equal of the "Jeeps" on sand and mud too—without the weight penalty!

Maybe this was the way of the future for Paris-Dakar?

I met with Yoshio Takaoka and Noriyuki Koseki from Subaru and they agreed that the light weight of the Subaru could well play a factor. They would provide me with two cars, one to be entered in the standard, (relatively) unmodified class; the other, which I would drive, to be entered in the prototype class. After I made a quick trip to Japan to work out the specifications, the cars eventually arrived in Brussels. Mine then underwent a couple of weeks of intense weight loss. Front fenders, hood, doors, and rear hatch were replaced with Kevlar parts; all the windows were replaced with plastic ones; and the entire heating and ventilation system was stripped out. When the car was ready to go, complete with all necessary extras such as long-range fuel tanks (though without the fuel in them), two spare wheels, emergency rations, and drinking water, it turned the scales at an incredible 750kg or 1,650lb!

We led the rally for the first week; across the Sahara Desert and down into Mali the little Subaru just flew from bump to bump, while the big, heavy, traditional off-roaders were destroying themselves. After leading for an exhilarating seven days, a fault in the fuel system eventually caused the car to catch fire and my codriver and I could only watch as it burned away to almost nothing. We hitched a ride on the "sweeper" truck into Gao in Mali, to be greeted with the news that my other "standard" car had also had a fire, but although out of the rally, was still a runner. The other Subaru drivers elected air travel for the remainder of the trip, which was fine by me. Feeling frustrated and disappointed by the fire, which had perhaps robbed us of victory, I just wanted some time alone with my thoughts—and Africa. I loaded the standard car with provisions and then drove it

Porsche 911 Rally, Paris-Dakar, 1984
*Porsche heads for victory on the Paris-Dakar Rally with
the car that was the forerunner of the fabulous 959.*
Werkfoto Porsche

alone, camping out and sleeping under the stars,
to Dakar, arriving just in time to meet the winners.

Obviously my analysis of the weight problem
did not go unnoticed, as two years later Porsche
brought three lightweight, all-wheel-drive 911-
based racers to Paris-Dakar and finished first and
second with what was, in fact, the forerunner of
the fabulous 959.

Jumping the Car

We have already seen how important balance
is in braking, steering, and accelerating. Another

feature of understanding and controlling the balance of the car also comes into play in off-road driving: the ability to *lift* the car over what might otherwise be damaging obstacles.

Imagine you are driving along an off-road
track at 50 or 60mph when ahead you see a gully
across the road, wide enough and deep enough
that you do not want the front wheels to drop into
it. It is too close to be able to stop. What can you
do?

You can use the front to rear, up and down
balance of the vehicle. Remember that when you
are braking heavily there is a weight transfer to-

ward the front of the car and as you accelerate, there is a similar weight transfer toward the rear? Now you are going to use *both* of them to get yourself out of trouble.

First, brake as hard as possible. Don't worry about locking up the wheels; whether or not they are locked will have little effect on your stopping distance in these conditions. With the brakes hard on, there will be a massive weight transfer toward the front and you will keep the brakes on until the moment *before* reaching the gully, tree trunk, or whatever is there. At the instant just before you would hit, snap off the brake pedal and go instantly to the throttle pedal. Just coming off the brakes will cause a weight transfer to the rear; getting on the throttle pedal instantaneously will amplify it

and, quite literally, help to *lift* the front of the car over the obstacle.

Night Driving

Driving at night creates problems for many people and, for anyone with less-than-perfect eyesight, can be traumatic. For those of us who are lucky enough to have almost perfect eyes, driving at night can be a pleasure, but again, you must be prepared.

Clean windows, of course, and good light selection with clean lenses are a must. If your car is a nonsmoking car, the inside probably stays reasonably clean. However, if you smoke in the car, be aware that smoking builds up an opaque film on the inside of the glass fairly quickly, so be pre-

Braking hard, top, will load up the front end. Snapping off the brake and onto the throttle, bottom, will allow the front wheels to "lift."

Porsche 911, Stuttgart-Lyon-Charbonnières, 1967
*I found this to be the ideal lighting setup for European ral-
lies where much of the competitive driving is done at night.
Headlights on the outside, then the foglights, then the
long-range spotlights in the center. Here I am on the way
to the Lyon-Charbonnières victory.* Vic Elford collection

pared to clean it often. Again, many proprietary products exist for cleaning the glass, but the best way is probably still the plain, damp, old-fashioned chamois leather.

It is difficult to prescribe the "ideal" light setup, and it may even depend on local highway and traffic laws. My personal choice was to use standard high-quality asymmetric headlights such as Bosch, Cibié, or Marchal, backed up by a matched pair of foglights and two long-range spotlights.

A little trick I discovered for driving on rally stages at night was to reverse the asymmetric setting of one of the headlights. I would use a left-hand-drive car headlight on the right side of the car and a right-hand-drive car headlight on the left side. Then instead of having the sharp cutoff of the dipped lights both angled the same way, the right one would be angled along the right side of the road and the left one along the left side.

In the photo, the long-range lights—the two nearest the center of the car—are set to project a powerful tunnel of light into the distance, beyond the reach of the headlights. The headlights provide all the illumination needed for the middle distance, and you will note that the foglights are turned outward a little, so that they are literally shining around corners. They are wired so that I can use any pair individually, or any combination of all three pairs together. The long-range lamps are also wired through a double switch so that they can be on independently or connected through the dip switch so that they only come on when the headlight main beams are on.

All of them have 60- or even 75-watt bulbs, which are probably illegal for normal highway use in most places. If you are able to use such high-output lighting, remember that the standard alternator may not be able to cope, and you might need to fit a heavy-duty one.

Whatever you do, don't use your headlights the way they did in Greece the first time I went there for the Acropolis Rally in 1958. Maybe they had dip switches that did not work, or perhaps nobody had ever learned their function, but when Greek drivers encountered another car coming toward them, one driver would switch his or her lights *off* for about five seconds, while the other stayed on high beam. Then, as if by telepathy, they would reverse the situation, and so on...and so on.... Needless to say, those of us for whom this was a new and novel approach were never able to get the synchronization right the way the Greeks did!

Driving in Fog

There is an ongoing debate over whether you can see better in fog with yellow lights or with white ones. I personally believe that pure white is

best as it gives a more natural light than yellow, particularly in fog associated with rain or snow, where the yellow ones throw horrendous, distorted shadows.

But whichever ones you prefer, how you use them is important. The long-range lights should be off as they will cause a blinding glare in front of you. The foglights, of course, should be on and they should be of the flat-top cutoff-type beam that can really reach out underneath the fog. Use the headlights in the dipped position, but every few seconds flick them up to main beam, and you will find that you can get a series of almost slow motion glimpses of what the road is doing ahead. Flicking your eyes up and down with the headlights will also help you avoid getting mesmerized and sleepy.

One thing that most people forget is that fog is damp. I am frequently amazed at drivers who peer vainly into the fog through a misty windshield. You must keep the wipers going to keep the screen clear—either intermittently, continuously, or with frequent bursts of washer/wiper.

Porsche 911, Monte Carlo Rally, 1968
Although this photo was taken in daylight, you can see how the foglights are angled outward, so they literally shine round the corners. This was my car on the way to winning the Monte Carlo Rally. Vic Elford collection

135

The conventional, slow way around a corner.

Driving on Ice, Snow, or Gravel

Driving on ice and snow or on smooth graded gravel roads can be an immense source of pleasure, but you need a lot of practice to obtain proficiency. Take the example shown in the accompanying diagram, which might be a typical downhill hairpin bend, covered in ice and snow, on the Monte Carlo Rally.

Even if your car is equipped with excellent studded snow tires it will still be limited in its ability to slow down as you brake. As in the rain, its grip around corners will also be drastically reduced, so there is only one way to negotiate the corner "conventionally." First you must brake smoothly a long way from the corner in order to slow down. Remember from the chapter on tires that snow tires are usually narrower than those used on a dry road. They have to be, in order to apply the maximum amount of pressure to dig into the snow and provide grip, so the frontal tire area in contact with the surface is comparatively small. The braking efficiency here is not limited by the power of the brakes—you could easily lock the wheels by using more force—but by the friction from the contact area on the road.

When you arrive at the turning point for the corner, your speed will only be about, say, 10mph, otherwise you would simply slide off the road. You must drive all the way around the corner, from 'A,' at a constant speed, and you cannot get back on the power until you are pointing in a straight line again at 'B.' This means that from 'A' to 'B' you were neither slowing down nor speeding up, which from a competition point of view, was time wasted.

But there is a way to slow down more effectively, to carry more speed into the corner, and then to accelerate much earlier. In order for it to work, the car, if it is rear-wheel drive, must have a limited-slip rear differential.

First, as you approach the corner you turn the car sideways, which will probably double the friction patch being used to slow the car. Contrary to what you might expect, you do not turn the car sideways so it is facing *into* the corner, but so that it is facing *away* from the corner.

Then with careful balance of brake pedal and steering wheel, you hold the car at approximately the angle shown until you arrive at the turning point, which you can approach at a much higher speed than in the "conventional" method above.

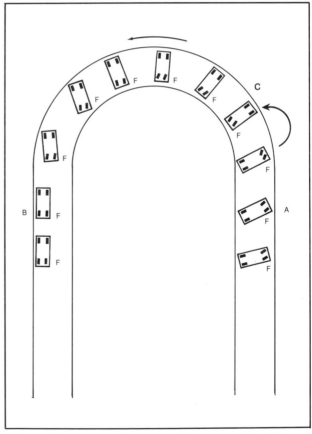

The quick way around a corner. You approach at 'A' very fast with the car sliding sideways facing away from the corner, the 'F' signifying the front of the car. At 'A' you overcorrect and the car will start to spin. At 'C' you steer into the new skid. The power is hard on to keep the car on the road.

The speed at point 'A' in the first case is probably only about 10mph, where in the second case it might be about 40mph.

Now as you approach the corner, the car is actually sliding to its left, so the steering wheel is turned slightly in that direction—steering into the skid. At point 'A,' flick the wheel hard to the left, in other words, *overcorrecting* the slide. Remember from our control, pause, and recovery exercise, overcorrecting is going to make the rear of the car come around the other way, so here the car will swing around its pivot point (chapter 4). As soon as it starts to swing you must start to turn the steering wheel the other way, so that by the time the car reaches 'C,' where it is now sliding to the right, you are already steering into the skid to the right.

But when the car started to rotate at 'A,' it was still going much too fast to get around the corner. The brakes are now off and you are not slowing down. The only way to slow the car now and avoid going off the road backward *is to use the power!* So, push hard on the throttle now, which will have the effect of pushing the car back in toward the inside of the corner. Now, by carefully balancing the power with the amount of steering being applied, you can actually start accelerating out of the corner from point 'C' much earlier that in the conventional way where you had to wait to get to point 'B.'

The first time I saw this technique used was in the Chartreuse mountains in France, doing tire tests for the Monte Carlo Rally at night. It was in my early days driving for Ford, and I was due to drive a Cortina GT in the rally. Ford had also entered three monstrous American Ford Galaxies, one of which would be driven by one of the great Swedish exponents of winter driving at that time, Bo Ljungfeld. Having heard about the legendary ability of the Scandinavians on ice and snow, I volunteered to ride with Bo as I hoped to learn something from him. He knew by heart the few miles of road we were using, up one side of the mountain and down the other, so there was no need to read "pace notes"; I could just sit back and enjoy the ride.

Unfortunately, my enjoyment was somewhat limited, as I had never been so frightened in my life! Going up was not *too* bad, although the speed at which Bo approached and took the corners left me breathless. Once over the top and on the way down to the first series of corners, I was honestly convinced that he had suffered some sort of attack and was about to take the car and its occupants to oblivion. But after a few corners taken as above, I started to relax a little, realizing that he did, in fact, know exactly what he was doing, even in the big unwieldy Ford.

I spent the next couple of years learning to drive like that on slippery surfaces so that when the opportunity came to exploit the possibilities of the Porsche 911, I was ready for it.

I mentioned earlier that the 911 has an evil reputation for its handling ability on slippery surfaces.But this reputation is entirely undeserved.

The Porsche 911 is *the best* handling two-wheel-drive car in the world on slippery surfaces, providing it has the right tires. Because its pivot point is so far forward, you can literally steer it with the throttle, but as I said in chapter 2, you have to move and react *very* quickly so as to always keep the rear end under control.

Neither steering from the 3 o'clock and 9 o'clock positions nor shuffle steering works in these conditions, because neither is fast enough. You have to literally spin the wheel with one hand, then catch it and stop it with the other at the right moment.

In the cornering situation described above, one of the reasons the Porsche 911 is so good is because there is so much weight over the rear wheels, giving it a great pendulum effect and tremendous traction when it is time to apply the power.

The only other car capable of challenging the 911 was the Renault Alpine A110, but the Alpine was small and had few of the creature comforts of the Porsche. It was strictly a sports car whose primary function in life was competition, whereas the Porsche was built as a fast, comfortable, long-distance Grand Touring car for two with all their luggage.

Long after I had learned to drive like Bo, someone asked not only how it was done, but how it worked. Frankly, I had no idea, but having been an engineer, I like solving problems, so I sat down with a paper and pencil and figured it out.

In fact, it is simple and revolves around the triangle of forces. Any force acting on an object can be represented as a linear vector on paper. By linear vector I mean that both the direction and the size of the force can be shown by one single line. When two forces are acting on an object, the resultant single force is represented by the third line needed to close the triangle.

In figure A, the forces acting on the car are caused by its momentum, F1, and the braking effect of the tires, F2, so the resultant is FR.

In figure B, the forces are F1, still due to the initial momentum, and F2, due to the power being applied to the rear wheels. The resultant is FR and at this instant the car is traveling exactly in the direction of the arrow FR.

As the car goes around the corner, the momentum as well as the amount and direction of the force being applied by the rear wheels are all constantly changing. At any given instant there is an F1, an F2, and therefore, an FR. If you were to

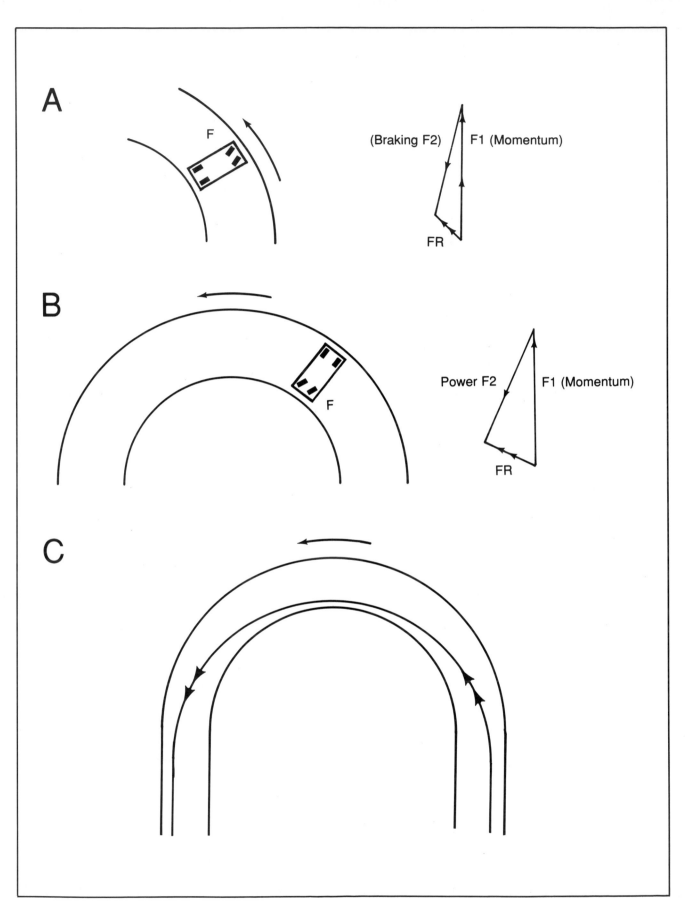

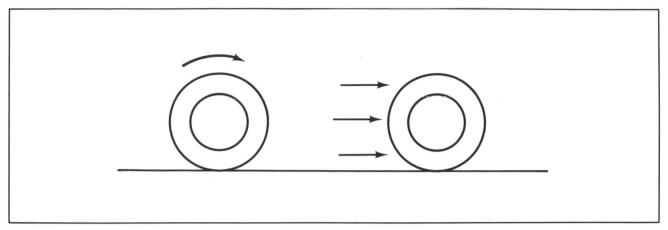

Between the point where the wheel is rolling freely and the point where it is locked, there is an instant when it has both braking and grip.

take the infinite number of FR arrows and connect them, you would finish with the line followed by the car around the corner as shown in figure c.

Once you understand the principle and have mastered the technique, you can use this skill to adjust the angle of the car even when the corner opens or tightens.

In the corner shown, the car is carefully balanced with a mixture of power and steering: the steering being into the skid, also known as opposite lock steering.

If the car is at the absolute limit of speed and adhesion all the way from 'A' to 'B' where the corner tightens up, how can you slow down and turn the car enough to avoid going off the road?

By unwinding the steering a little—in other words, turning the wheel *into* the corner—you will have a larger side contact area presented by the front tires to provide friction, and the rear of the car will want to slide out further. Depending on the surface, you may have to lift off the throttle pedal for an instant, creating the trailing throttle oversteer that you learned about earlier—but be ready to get back on the throttle the instant the car has started to rotate.

Driving on Black Ice

If the road is *really* slippery, just adding more power as the steering is turned may send the rear of the car out from under you, and again, you must be ready to apply instant correction the moment the car starts rotating.

Back in chapter 9 I said that there is one, just one, situation where "cadence braking" works. That is when you are confronted by sheet ice or black ice and you have virtually no grip at all. There is probably not a driver alive who is sufficiently sensitive to be able to squeeze the brakes on without locking the wheels on sheet ice. Even

the ABS can get confused. Because there is so little resistance, it "thinks" the car has stopped. If you just lock the brakes, the car will eventually slow down, but as anyone who has ever experienced that heart-stopping moment in such conditions knows, it seems to take forever.

By stabbing on and off the brakes as fast as possible you will stop a lot sooner than just sitting there with the wheels locked. As with everything involved in the dynamics of driving, there is a simple physical reason for this. Let's just look at what happens at one wheel. Each time you put your foot on the brake the wheel will go from a free-rolling state to a locked state where it is just sliding on the ice. Conversely, as you take your foot off the brake, it will go from being locked to rolling freely. Logic tells you that during each transition from rolling to locked and from locked to rolling, there is a tiny moment when there is both braking and friction, so during that moment, the car is slowing down. Since those moments are very tiny indeed, you need to create as many of them as possible, so the faster you can pump your foot up and down on the brake pedal, the quicker you will stop. Force is of no importance, you obviously do not need much to lock the wheels on ice; the speed with which you move your foot *is* of importance.

This is another of those little exercises you can try on a deserted parking lot on Sunday morning. You don't have to be going fast; 10mph will do. Lock the wheels up at that speed and see how far you slide before coming to a stop. Then do it again with the pumping action and see how much shorter the stopping distance is. You will actually feel the little jerk each time the wheels go through the friction moment.

You have already seen that whatever the conditions, the car will always react to a direct input from the driver. This applies whether the input is voluntary or not. If you suddenly encounter sheet ice, the automatic reaction is to lift off the throttle pedal, which is a direct input from the driver. Even on ice, because of the dynamics going on within the car itself, there will be a weight transfer, which will almost certainly result in a spin. Instead of just lifting off the gas pedal, it is preferable to lift off the gas pedal and *at the same time* declutch, or push the clutch pedal in, so that the car is rolling absolutely freely. Now the only input the driver can make is with the steering, which must be done, of course, with extreme smoothness, but with which *it may* be possible to steer out of trouble.

Such a situation happened to me once in Europe. Thanks to my friend Ferdinand Piëch, I owned the first five-cylinder Audi 100 car sold in Belgium. Early one winter morning, I turned off the freeway and was taking the long, sweeping exit ramp at about 90mph, when looking ahead I started to see puffs of dust, which I quickly discovered were being caused by cars hitting and bouncing off guard rails! Although the freeway had been clear, the exit ramp ran over a bridge and was covered with black ice. Although I realized what was happening in front of me, I also knew that there was no way in the world I was going to be able to stop before I got there. By pushing the clutch in and immediately putting the gearbox in neutral I disconnected the engine and transmission from the wheels so that the car was simply freewheeling, and I was able, smoothly and delicately, to steer my way through the carnage that was going on around me. Like the trip over the Col de la Couillole on the way to winning "the Monte," it was a few moments before my nerves, and hands, were steady enough to light a cigarette!

Another technique that helps in slowing down on slippery roads is using both brake and throttle pedal *simultaneously*. It will work to a limited extent with rear-wheel drive, but really comes into its own with front-wheel drive and especially with four-wheel drive.

We already know that on packed snow or ice it is difficult to apply the brakes without locking up the wheels. However, it is logical that if you keep some power applied to the driven wheels it will be more difficult to lock them with the brakes.

With a front- or four-wheel-drive car, brake with the *left* foot but at the same time keep a little power applied with the right foot still on the throttle. Keeping the power on will prevent the driven wheels from locking—and the harder you brake, the more power you must apply—to avoid locking the wheels.

You can use the same technique with a rear-wheel-drive car, but only to slow down in a straight line, because with the front wheels undriven they are likely to lock up early and cause a loss of steering.

Chapter 12

Accident Avoidance

The place: Outside Lyon, France
The time: One rainy afternoon in 1974
The occasion: Waiting in line at a red light

I was sitting in my Porsche waiting patiently for the traffic light to change. As always when I am driving, my eyes were never still, but roaming around ahead, to the side, and even though I was stationary, still frequently glancing in the rearview mirror. One of these rearward glances showed a car approaching from behind at such a speed that it seemed evident that the driver had not seen the traffic sitting motionless in front of him. When he was about 100 yards away I decided that there was no way he was going to be able to stop and it was time to get out of the way. I had left about fourft between my car and the one in front and was able to squeeze past his rear fender and onto the grass shoulder beside the road. At that moment the oncoming driver suddenly realized that everyone was stopped, slammed on the brakes, and slid at about 40mph into the rear of the stationary car that I had left exposed!

Even while sitting still at a red light you can do some positive things to keep out of someone else's trouble. Had I been sitting there conducting blaring rock music with both hands, oblivious to all around me, my Porsche would have been going home on a tow truck. Always try to have an alternative to just staying where you are on the road and becoming involved in an avoidable accident.

The things I am going to say now will most certainly upset some people, but they are fundamentally true.

First, accidents, with rare exceptions, don't just happen, they are caused.

Second, speed in itself does not kill.

Accidents Are Caused

Accidents are usually caused by a mistake of some sort. Inattention, lack of anticipation, poor judgment, lack of awareness of what is going on around you—all are human faults for which you are responsible.

You can avoid accidents by looking for every little telltale sign that might indicate that something unexpected is about to happen. That way, when it does, it is no longer unexpected, but *anticipated*. Some examples of telltale signs are: the ball bouncing into the road that is almost certainly going to be followed by its small owner, oblivious to the danger; the tiny pair of feet glimpsed underneath a parked car that might take off in any direction; the car approaching fast down a side road that probably won't be able to stop before it gets to the main road; the vehicle in front of you that is wandering along with its driver looking for house numbers or street names; the woman putting on her makeup or the man shaving with the aid of the inside mirror; the dog rushing across the road in front of you that will probably be followed by one or more of its species.

Accidents, with rare exceptions, don't just happen, they are caused.

All of these situations are potential hazards and might create a situation that could lead to an accident. You cannot control those events, of course, but by being aware of them you can avoid the accident situations that they may lead to.

Give the guy looking for street names a couple of extra car lengths space, so that if he does suddenly find what he is looking for and turns left just in front of you, you have time to stop. Slow down the moment you see that bouncing ball so that when its owner does appear at full speed you have already virtually stopped. Not only will you not run over the child, but you will also protect him or

141

her from the vehicles behind whose drivers were not so forward thinking as you. Practice again the running commentary we talked about in chapter 3, analyzing all the potential accident situations you see.

Controlling Your Speed

Speed in itself does not kill. But the wrong speed at the wrong time very often does kill. I'm still alive despite having driven down the Mulsanne straight at Le Mans many, many times at over 240mph. Of course, had I made a mistake at that speed it is quite possible I would not be here today.

Speed in itself does not kill. But the wrong speed at the wrong time very often does kill.

In Germany, driving your Porsche for long distances at 120–150mph on the autobahn is perfectly normal. That is what both Porsches and autobahns were built for. Both the Porsche driver and the driver in the little Ford cruising along in the slow lane at a mere 70mph are used to the speed discrepancy, and *each respects the other*. Each has a responsibility to the other and each must exercise the anticipation we talked about in chapter 3. When the Porsche driver sees the little car closing up behind a heavy truck on an upgrade, he *expects* him to pull out to overtake. When the Ford driver sees a Porsche coming up behind him in his mirror, he *expects* the Porsche to be going fast so he avoids darting out in front of it unexpectedly.

How often have you been overtaken in a 30mph zone by a car driven at 40–45mph, weaving in and out of traffic with little thought for other road users, only to come up behind the same car a few minutes later, out on the open highway, still doing only 45mph, but now getting in everyone's way?

Accidents are usually caused by a mistake of some sort: inattention, lack of anticipation, poor judgment, lack of awareness of what is going on around you—all are human faults for which you are responsible.

Everyone has different skill levels; everyone has different reaction times. Some people have more natural balance and feeling than others and can drive much faster on slippery surfaces. Some people have better eyesight and can drive quicker at night. The important thing is to learn and know your own limits under all conditions and, just in case something does go wrong, *always wear your safety belt*.

Falling off the third rung of a stepladder can kill you, although if that happens, your head will only be doing about 17mph when it hits the ground! Like everything else in driving, your speed, however high or low it may be, must be controlled.

Chapter 13

Competition Driving

The place: Somewhere in the French Alps
The time: 4a.m., one morning in 1967
The occasion: The Tulip Rally

There was a terrible bang and the crunch of folding metal as the right front fender of the Porsche 911 hit the rough unyielding rock face and ground to a halt with a punctured front tire.

Wearing "number one" on the car, David Stone and I had been the first to leave Noordwijk on the Dutch coast two days earlier at the start of the Dutch International Tulip Rally. The first special stage, which was also the only one held in The Netherlands, had been at the Zandvoort racetrack. From The Netherlands, the rally headed south into the French Alps where most of the competi-

Porsche 911, Tulip Rally, 1967
I take the 911 off the line of a special stage on the way to the Tulip Rally victory. Look at the concentration in the eyes. Foster and Skeffington Ltd.

Porsche 911, Tulip Rally, 1967
My pristine 911 on one of the earlier special stages of the
same Tulip Rally.... Foster and Skeffington Ltd.

tive driving would take place. We had set the fastest time at Zandvoort, as we had on every single special stage since, and had built up a substantial lead.

Now it seemed as though all that effort might have been for nothing. Being number one was a great advantage on all the special stages, as it meant that there was never anyone in front of us who might cost us precious seconds while we overtook them. Unfortunately, it also meant that we were the first car on the road and would be the first to encounter any unexpected hazards.

We had just encountered one! Coming out of a tunnel high in the mountains on what was a fairly straightforward road section (or liaison section) between special stages, I had found the road covered in sheet ice. Having just come from a dry hill climb, the car was on racing tires, which have virtually no grip at all on ice, and I had simply slid straight into the rock face. (We were going much too fast for cadence braking to have any appreciable effect in the distance available.)

At first glance the damage appeared light—a punctured tire and bent front bumper and fender—and since it was on a liaison section we were not too pressed for time. We changed the wheel but found that the bumper was still rubbing on the tire. It was then that we discovered just how strongly Porsches were built: trying to prize the bumper away from the wheel with our hands and a hammer was like trying to kill an elephant with a fly swatter!

Fortunately there was a convenient telephone pole right there and we were able to attach one end of the tow rope to it and the other end to the bumper. After numerous attempts, jerking the car backward until the rope threatened to break and the telephone pole quivered ominously above us, we managed to get the bumper away from the wheel.

All this had taken time, of course, and when we reached the next time control, we were three minutes late. Somehow David managed to check in discreetly at the time control without any of the

144

competitors being aware of our time loss. (Time lost on road sections, or liaison sections, was one minute for every minute or part thereof and total time on special stages was measured in seconds.) This meant that I would have to make up three minutes over the next fastest competitor on the special stages.

I talked earlier about my special relationship with Hermann Briem and Huschke von Hanstein—now all that mutual trust was coming into play. I had calculated, from my knowledge of the special stages, that I needed only a maximum speed of 100mph. By using equally spaced gears and a *very* low final-drive ratio, it was possible to build such a transmission, but Hermann was worried that the low final-drive ratio, being essentially one developed for short sprint races, would not survive 2,500 miles of road use and numerous wheel-spinning hill climb starts. Fortunately I had convinced him that by being gentle and smooth, I would make it last. Now we were able to take advantage of the luxury of gears that were not avail-

able to other manufacturers and that even other Porsche drivers had not dared to try.

The first stage after the accident was a hill climb up the Mont Salève, just south of Geneva, and in a six minute climb we beat the next car, which incidentally was another Porsche 911, by half a minute!

Around Geneva to the north side of the city—all this through liaison sections on roads in France since the Swiss are not fond of motor sport—to the Col de la Faucille. There we not only beat all our competitors but also beat the *outright* hill climb record set only the year before by a Formula 2 car in the European Hill Climb Championship!

One particular corner on the way up will live forever in my memory. As I exited a long right-hander absolutely on the limit at about 75mph, there was a solitary gendarme standing at the edge of the road in front of a low stone wall. He had nowhere to go but backward over the wall and that was my last view of him as he disappeared down among the trees.

Porsche 911, Tulip Rally, 1967
...And my 911 looking rather second-hand after it's rock bashing and marker bashing episodes, which had little

effect on an overwhelming victory. Foster and Skeffington Ltd.

Porsche 908/3, Nürburgring, 1971
Even during a pit stop, concentration can be vitally important.... Vic Elford collection

David and I continued this hectic pace throughout the next day and night, slowly getting back the three minutes we had lost. At one point we had a *downhill* stage in the Alsace mountains, and even there we were able to make the fastest time, beating Timo Makinen's Mini Cooper S by one second.

The last real road stage was a hill climb at yet another European Hill Climb Championship venue, La Roche-Samrée in Belgium. Traveling very fast, the last two left-hand corners taking us right to the limit of our 100mph top speed, we went through the first one with no problem, but as I turned into the second, nothing happened—the car wanted to go straight on. I slowed, braked, and wound on more and more steering, but we were still heading for the trees. I finally got the car to

respond a little, but not before it had taken out a number of the little concrete reflector markers on the outside of the corner, with a series of bing bing bings as it mowed them down.

Our momentum helped carry us to the finish line and after having our time recorded—despite the problems, we were still fastest—we surveyed the damage: both right side tires punctured and a lot of crumpled bodywork. Obviously the right front tire puncturing had been responsible for the loss of steering, and the rear one had been punctured on the concrete markers.

Now we had another major problem: Our next service point was after the next special stage as we had not anticipated the need for service here, and we had only one spare wheel. While we pondered our dilemma, we changed one wheel and waited for the next Porsche 911 driver to arrive. When he did, I explained our predicament and asked him to lend me his spare wheel, on the understanding that I would run behind him until we came to the next service point. If he needed the wheel back I would give it to him and my rally would be over.

Competition driving is like any other form of competition. You must have the ability, the dedication, and will to succeed, and allied to all of that, the concentration.

I cannot, for the life of me, remember who that driver was. I know he wasn't an Englishman, but he was most certainly a gentleman and agreed. We both made it safely to the next service, and David and I continued setting fastest times everywhere, finally winning the rally by forty-six seconds over Timo Makinen, which meant that we had been three minutes and forty-six seconds faster than him on the special stages!

Porsche 908/3, Nürburgring, 1971
...As it can be while waiting for the car to arrive. Vic Elford collection

Porsche 908/3, Nürburgring, 1971
Moments after the start of the 1971 Nürburgring 1000km. In my Porsche 908/3 number 3, I would eventually dispose of Jacky Ickx, number 15 Ferrari, and Rolf

Stommelen, number 16 Alfa Romeo, for my third victory in the event, this time with Gerard Larrousse. Vic Elford collection

Nürburgring, 1971
Gerard and I celebrate in victory lane.... Vic Elford collection

Nürburgring, 1971
...And the celebrations continue. Vic Elford collection

Concentration

Competition driving is like any other form of competition. You must have the ability, the dedication, and will to succeed, and allied to all of that, the *concentration*.

Remember the Sebring twelve hours that I won with Gerard Larrousse, where he kept his concentration all the way to the end of the race and then when it was no longer needed, he relaxed it and spun on the cooling-down lap?

Even funnier, at least for those watching, was the cool-down lap of Italian Vittorio Brambilla, who won a rain-shortened Austrian Grand Prix at Zeltweg. With Zeltweg being only a few hours from northern Italy, thousands of his compatriots had swarmed across the border to watch him. He was so excited at winning in front of them that as a result of his enthusiastic waving to the crowd he crashed heavily. It was a good five minutes before he appeared at the pit entrance with the car looking like some sort of demented mechanical crab, hauling itself along sideways with only two wheels touching the ground.

Once you have decided that a competition driving career is for you, be aware that to succeed, whether it be at an amateur level or with the intention of making it through the ranks to Indy-Cars or Formula 1, you have to be prepared to sac-

Lola 212, Nürburgring
I had a great affinity with the Nürburgring. Here I was on the way to winning my second consecutive 500km, this time in a Lola 212. On both occasions I was the only

driver to drive all twenty-two laps of the tortuous 14-mile circuit in the Eiffel mountains without a co-driver! Eberhard Strähle

rifice virtually everything else to get there. Like any top level sport, motor racing requires a great deal of single-mindedness to succeed.

Many years ago, when I was commuting regularly back and forth across the Atlantic to compete in Trans-Am and Can-Am, I cooperated in a psychological survey done by a scientific team from southern California to measure the ability of people to work under pressure. They tested many groups—amateur and professional racing drivers, businesspeople, and athletes from other sports—and came up with a startling discovery. People from every group eventually got to a point where their performance under increasing stress disintegrated—*except racing drivers, who continued to get better the more stress they were under!*

They also discovered something that anyone who is married to a racing driver could have told

Chaparral 2J, Laguna Seca, 1970
Concentration as I prepare to go to work for another pole position in Jim Hall's fabulous Chaparral 2J "vacuum cleaner." Dave Friedman

People from every group eventually got to a point where their performance under increasing stress disintegrated—except racing drivers, who continued to get better the more stress they were under!

them for free: that racing drivers in general were self-centered, had little need for conformism, and were driven only by what *they* considered to be a measure of success. Winning, to a racing driver, means everything. There are occasions when a driver is content to finish second—but they are rare.

Physical Preparation

We have discussed learning to drive and some of the basics in preparing the car to be driven, so let us look for a moment at preparing the *driver* for competition.

Chaparral 2J, Riverside, 1970
Here I am at Riverside with a bemused Mark Donohue looking on at the rear. Gary Bramstedt

Jogging is a popular way for many people to stay in shape, although I must admit that I tried it a few times and found it depressing and boring so I gave it up. I found that the best physical training for driving a racing car was driving a racing car. Developing your skills as a test driver, being able to understand what the car is doing and why, and then being able to transmit that information to your engineers will help you get plenty of seat time.

Most racing drivers have a natural aptitude for other sports, particularly those requiring balance and hand/eye coordination such as skiing, tennis, golf, swimming, and sailing, for example.

All of these form valid and enjoyable training programs. The same is true in reverse, incidentally. A couple of years ago I had the pleasure of teaching Martina Navratilova at a Porsche Owners Driving School and I doubt that I have ever seen anyone else with such ability to concentrate. Whatever the exercise, it never took her more than two tries to get it perfect. And years ago, just after his triple gold medal winter Olympics, I met Jean-Claude Killy. A few months later, driving in the Targa Florio—his first ever motor race—he won the GT category! In a Porsche 911. In my case, I scuba dive, which is excellent for concentration, alertness, and self-control.

Chaparral 2J, Road Atlanta, 1970
At speed at Road Atlanta with the "sucker car." Vic Elford collection

Jim Hall and myself in a pensive mood as we survey the opposition. Peter C. Borsari

There is, however, one part of your body that you will have to work on in the gym, and that is the neck muscles. They will need considerable development in order to be able to withstand the G forces generated by modern race cars. A good modern family car is probably capable of cornering at about 0.75 G, your Porsche can reach about 0.9 G, and before the advent of ground effects, race cars could develop around 1.3 G, maybe 1.5 G. With the evolution of ground effects, Indy cars now reach over 3.0 G, and a Formula 1 car can reach a staggering 4.5 G. In other words, a Formula 1 car can create five or six times the centrifugal force in a corner than the car you drive on the road! When you are cornering with that kind of force acting on you, it is the equivalent of having a bowling ball strapped to your head!

If you watch IndyCar racing you will notice that many of the drivers have a strap attached to their helmet with the other end connected to their shoulder or even to the car, so that the head can only move a limited distance. This is especially important on a short oval track like Phoenix where the cars are almost constantly cornering.

Whether you are about to take part in the Indy 500 or an SCCA club race, the Monte Carlo Rally or a Porsche Club slalom, you should lead up to the start in the same way. Plenty of sleep, not just the night before, but for many nights previously, helps build up stamina. Eating a good healthy diet will help build physical strength and keep your head clear. Please, no triple martini lunches or after-dinner cognacs. Years ago many drivers and other athletes used to smoke, but if you haven't started yet, the best advice I can give is, don't. I did—in fact I still do—but I don't recommend it.

Mental Preparation

When you set off for the event, allow for being stuck in traffic and make sure you have plenty of time to get there. Be sure that all your driving clothes are clean and fresh—nothing is more de-

McLaren, Road Atlanta, 1991
*Still active in vintage racing, here I am at speed at Road
Atlanta in my current mount, the beautifully restored
850hp Can-Am McLaren owned by Richard and Benton
Bryan.* Gordon L. Jolley

154

moralizing than having to put on the same damp, smelly fireproof underwear that you wore yesterday!

For the last hour or so before the start, concentrate on your mental preparation so that you reach the point of 100 percent concentration at the moment the flag drops or the green light comes on. How you do that will depend on your character. If you have an outgoing, gregarious nature, you might need constant contact and conversation during this time. Others might want to slowly tune out to what is going on around them. I belong to the second group and used to sit quietly in a corner of the garage blotting everything out so that when I finally got to the start line I had only one thing in mind—the start.

In fact, not many drivers have the ability to be instantly at 100 percent when the start is given. Looking back over recent years, only Jackie Stewart, Niki Lauda, Emerson Fittipaldi, Ayrton Senna, and Michael Andretti (in IndyCar racing) come immediately to mind as having that gift. Most of us are at perhaps 90–95 percent most of the time, if we are lucky.

Don't smoke.

Chapter 14

Putting It All Together

The place: San Francisco
The time: January 1991
The occasion: Lunch on Saturday

Porsche Cars North America had just received the first Porsche 911 Turbo of the 1991 model year. I was ready to leave Reno for a week of meetings, starting at Willow Springs racetrack, continuing on to San Diego, and then terminating in San Jose and San Francisco.

Brian Bowler, then president of Porsche Cars North America, asked me if I would mind taking the Turbo for my trip as I was the only one in the company who could really evaluate it from a performance point of view.

Would I mind?

The week's business over, I was sitting in Basta Pasta, one of my favorite San Francisco Italian restaurants with my wife Anita, who had done the trip with me and our two 6ft-tall teenagers. We had just picked them up from the airport, together with all their baggage from a month in Europe. Listening to the anecdotes of their vacation, enjoying the marvelous spaghetti, and occasionally gazing out of the window, it was a while before it dawned on me that the rain was falling in sheets over the city.

The rain! If it's raining in San Francisco it must be snowing in the Sierras! A quick trip to the pay phone and the California Highway Patrol confirmed that Interstate 80 over the Donner Pass was alternately open and closed, sometimes with chain controls and definitely with major delays. On the other hand, the pass to the south of Lake Tahoe, Route 50, was still open with no restrictions.

The bill paid, everyone, bags and all, were squeezed into the 911 Turbo, and we were soon on our way. A stop for another quick phone call at Sacramento confirmed that Route 50 was still open. We started to climb. It started to snow.

Eventually we encountered the dreaded chain control, which was now stopping all traffic. I wasn't worried about the driving part, in fact, I was looking forward to it. But I *was* worried about conning my way past the chain control, which, not without reason, I must admit, often assumes that everyone behind the wheel in winter is a moron.

The state trooper peered in the window from beneath his yellow oilskins.

"Is this a front-wheel-drive car?"

"No," I lied. "This is the new Turbo Four, brand new four-wheel-drive car from Porsche, and it has all-weather tires."

"OK man, go, go," he replied and waved us on our way.

So we went.

The 911 Turbo has a rather peculiar limited-slip differential that allows a maximum of 20 percent slip on acceleration but locks up at 100 percent on deceleration. The theory, admirable for the conditions for which it was designed, is that 100 percent lockup on deceleration will give added stability.

But it doesn't work on snow! This meant that going up we had no problem. The car was sideways most of the time but the rear wheels were locked together giving traction, which I was able to control by the amount of correction applied, or steering into the skid.

Going down was something else altogether. The stabbing on the brakes that we talked about earlier is fine in a straight line on a flat surface, but now we had a narrow road with a lot of camber and no real straights. Just lifting off the throttle pedal had the effect of locking up the rear differential, and the wheels would then immediately start sliding down the camber, putting the car sideways. The only thing to do in these circumstances is to push the clutch in so the car is freewheeling, steer it back straight again, stab the brake pedal a few times to slow down, and then blip the throttle and get it exactly right in order to let the clutch out with perfect engine/road speed coordination so the car is balanced again.

Then the moment the car is unbalanced by a bend or the camber of the road the whole thing starts all over again...and again...and again....

I was enjoying the challenge so much and my concentration was so intense that it was not until we reached home that I realized that one of the kids had not uttered a word the whole way and the other was white from fear! Anita, on the other hand, had found the trip as exhilarating as her days as a rally codriver years ago.

Putting it all together means remembering all the little things that you have learned from this book and all your other sources over the years and being able to pull out the one that counts...when it counts.

In the case above it meant making maximum use of the limited-slip differential to keep traction on the way up. Then on the way down, disconnecting the drivetrain to get steering control and using cadence braking to slow down.

Above all, it means keeping cool and analyzing what is happening from one moment to the next so that you always anticipate what will happen and never have to hurry for something unexpected.

I hope this book has interested, entertained, and above all, instructed you. Before you drive again, read it a second time and really retain the things that matter to you in whatever type of driving you do.

Then drive well. Drive safely. And buckle up!

Above all, performance driving means keeping cool and analyzing what is happening so that you always anticipate what will happen and never have to hurry for something unexpected.

Rally Pace Notes

The first ever rally pace notes were the brainchild of what was then the BMC (British Motor Corporation) team back in 1961. Budgets were not what they are now and even a manufacturer could not afford to send its entire team for a couple of weeks reconnaissance before an international rally.

BMC had entered no less than six cars for the Acropolis Rally in Greece: three Austin-Healey 3000s and three Minis. One crew was sent to go over the entire route, making navigation notes so that the rest of us would not get lost. At the same time they would devise a system that would at least give us an indication of which way the road went when we were driving flat out against the clock on the unknown special stages. This was particularly important in Greece as the rally was in May, and with the speed sections almost always on dirt roads, we would often be blinded by dust from the cars in front.

That first set of pace notes looked something like this:
• 400yds House Right
• 200yds Left to Tree then Right
• 500yds Slight Left
• 1/2mi Tree and House Hairpin Right
• 50yds Left
• 100yds Bad Right

In those days, "slight" simply meant that the corner was less severe than it appeared to the driver, "right" (or "left") meant that it was more or less as it appeared, and "bad right" meant that it was

sharper than it appeared. Pretty elementary, to say the least, but it was a start.

The notes were read by the codriver/navigator so that the driver knew what was coming, and they obviously helped from a safety point of view, because at least we knew if the road went left or right, but they did not really help us go much quicker. Besides which, the navigator had to shout to be heard so he was likely to be hoarse or even speechless by the end of the rally.

Pace notes stayed fairly rudimentary for about two years until David Stone and I started thinking about how we could use them to actually go faster. Over the next few years we developed and refined the system until by 1968, when I quit rallying to concentrate on circuit racing, a typical section of my pace notes for the Monte Carlo Rally might have looked like this:
• 100 SR—SL • KR—L + R • KL into BR—FL + FR • 50 SR into L—Fast KR • Flat R—FL over Crest •
Flat over Crest bearing R • 100 Flat R—FL •
L into BR—HL—SR + over Crest • Long L tightens—R opens •
SL—SR—SR into OHL—Fast KR opens to SL •

Translation: Straight 100 Slight Right then Slight Left Straight Kay Right then Left and Right Straight Kay Left into Bad Right then Fast Left and Fast Right Straight 50 Slight Right into Left then Fast Kay Right Straight Flat Right then Fast Left over Crest Straight Flat over Crest Bearing Right [not really turning right, just aiming toward where the right side of the road would be after the crest] Straight 100 Flat Right then Fast Left Straight <u>Left into Bad Right</u> then <u>Hairpin Left</u> then Slight Right andover Crest Straight Long Left tightens then Right opens Straight Slight Left then Slight Right then <u>Slight Right into Open Hairpin Left</u> then Fast Kay Right opens to Slight Left Straight....

Code	Meaning
•	Straight (straight up to about 30 yards)
• 50	Straight 50 (straight 30–70 yards)
• 100	Straight 100 (straight 70–120 yards)
—	Then (ties the two corners together)
+	And (same as then, but even closer)

The corner codes in order of severity:

R

Right.

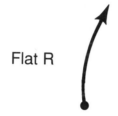

Flat R

Flat Right. Just that: flat out.

Long R

Long Right.

SR

Slight Right.

BR

Bad Right. Underlined so there is no chance of missing it.

FR

Fast Right.

HR

Hairpin Right. Underlined so there is no chance of missing it.

KR

Kay Right. Why "Kay"? No reason, except that we wanted a single syllable that stood out and could not be confused with any other word.

OHR

Open Hairpin Right. Underlined so there is no chance of missing it.

Of course, other combinations can be used, as shown in the example.

The real secret to using the notes was to have a codriver who was a pretty good driver in his or her own right, so that without even looking at the road ahead, he or she could *feel* what the car was doing and give the driver just the right amount of information each time it was needed and as far ahead as necessary. Advance notice is very important, for, as you can imagine, going downhill on ice and snow at 120mph the driver needs to know well in advance if there is a hairpin coming up!

As you can see, the notes now covered just about every configuration of road imaginable. Because we had developed this system together over the years, I could in theory drive absolutely flat out over a stage for which David had made the notes and which I had never seen before. In fact, that wasn't just theory. On the Tour de France—the one that used to exist for race cars, not the bicycle one—we had a special stage in the Pyrenees mountains. I had been unable to take the time to practice it, and David had made the pace notes alone. The stage took place at dawn; it was foggy and raining, and the road was covered in slippery wet clay. Not the ideal conditions for the big, brutal Ferrari 365 GTB/4 Daytona that I was driving, but relying totally on David and the notes he had made, I set the fastest time.

By now we were also using a fairly sophisticated intercom built into the crash helmets so there was no need to shout. The navigator could just sit back relaxed and speak in a normal voice. However, for that Tour de France, which was a one-off comeback rally for me, the Ferrari Daytona was so shatteringly noisy that even the normal intercom wasn't much use. Luckily, David had recently been to give a talk to his local Navy Air Base in England and in return for carrying "Fly Navy" stickers on the side of the car, the Navy lent us two fighter pilot helmets with throat microphones—the ultimate luxury as words were transmitted by vocal cord vibrations not by sound. A far cry from my wife Anita's early "intercom" innovation using a funnel and length of plastic hose piped into the driver's helmet so that he could hear what she was saying!

A few years later I went back to East Africa for the Safari Rally with the Subaru team and took the pace notes even further. Not only did they give corner-by-corner coverage, they also described the roughness of the terrain, which in Africa, also has a bearing on how fast you can drive without destroying the car. They looked like this:

SL + SR + SL—KR onto Rough 3 • L- R • 100
• over Crest onto Rough 2—SR + SL •
HR—L into SLOW Rough 1—SR to STOP Rough 0 for 50 yards—
L onto Smooth—SR—SL into KR + L—BR •
100 Flat over Crest bearing L onto rough 5 •
Translation:

The designation of the corners is exactly as before and the roughness of the road is on a sliding scale as follows:

Rough 5 is simply to warn the driver that it is coming, there is no need to slow down.

Rough 4 means slow down a little as the car will get a little unbalanced.

Rough 3 means slow down considerably.

Rough 2 means really slow down as the road is rough enough to do severe damage.

Rough 1 means virtually stop and look because it is so rough.

STOP Rough 0 means literally stop and look before proceeding. It might be used because of deep gullies, rocks, downed trees, or anything that is out of sight on the approach, over a crest, or around a bend.

Index